# Bunyan-ul-Marsoos

*Pakistan's Silent Thunder*

# Table of Content

**Chapter 1 The Strike That Woke the Nation**............................3

    The Pahalgam Incident: Catalyst of Conflict ................4

    Indian Missile Attacks on Pakistani Bases ...................7

    Civilian Panic and Military Readiness ........................10

**Chapter 2 Enter Bunyan-ul-Marsoos** ...................................14

    Naming the Mission: Meaning and Significance ........15

    Formation of a Unified Response Strategy .................18

    Faith as a Foundation for Action .................................21

**Chapter 3 Strategic Calculations**..........................................25

    Balancing Retaliation with Restraint............................26

    Briefings at GHQ and Air Force Command.................29

    Coordination Between Army, Air Force, and Intelligence.........32

**Chapter 4 Precision in the Sky** ............................................36

    Target Selection: Beyond Symbolism .........................37

    Drone Surveillance and Recon Flights ........................40

    Coordinated Air Strikes Begin .....................................43

**Chapter 5 Breaking the Myth of Invincibility** .....................48

    Strike on Pathankot and Adampur...............................49

BrahMos Storage Sites: A Tactical Blow .................................. 52

Neutralizing S-400 Air Defense Zones ................................... 56

## Chapter 6 The Invisible War: Cyber & EW ........................... 60

Cyber Disruption of Indian Grids and Comms ...................... 61

Electronic Warfare: Jammed and Blinded ............................. 64

ISI's Role in Info Ops ............................................................ 68

## Chapter 7 Civilian Shield, Military Spear ............................. 72

Protecting Urban Centers During Escalation ......................... 73

Internal Security Measures and Unity .................................... 76

Media Management and Public Morale ................................. 80

## Chapter 8 Global Eyes, Global Pressure .............................. 84

India's Diplomatic Moves at the UN ...................................... 85

Pakistan's Allies and the OIC Response ................................ 89

US, China, and Russia: Silent Observers ............................... 92

## Chapter 9 The Ceasefire Equation ....................................... 97

International Mediation Behind the Curtain .......................... 98

Strategic Pause: Calculated or Conceded? ........................... 102

Messages Sent, Lessons Learned .......................................... 105

## Chapter 10 Youm-e-Tashakur: A Nation Honors ............... 110

May 16 Declared Day of Gratitude ...................................... 111

Stories of Pilots and Ground Heroes ................................... 114

Military Honors and National Awards ..................................... 118

## Chapter 11 Psychological & Military Impact ..................... 122

A Doctrine of Deterrence Reasserted ....................................... 123

Indian Media and Political Fallout .......................................... 126

Global Reassessment of South Asian Dynamics ...................... 130

## Chapter 12 Lessons for the Future ......................................... 135

The Power of Measured Force ................................................ 136

Building on Technological and Tactical Success ..................... 140

Strengthening National Defense Policy .................................. 144

# Introduction

In early 2025, South Asia stood at a deceptive crossroads. While decades of friction between Pakistan and India simmered beneath the surface, the region appeared outwardly calm. Border skirmishes were frequent but normalized, and diplomatic channels—though tense—remained open. To the average observer, this was just another year of uneasy peace. Yet in the intelligence circles and military planning rooms, there was a growing sense of unease—an awareness that something was shifting beneath the surface, building quietly toward confrontation.

That silence shattered with the tragic incident in Pahalgam, where a deadly attack claimed the lives of many innocent civilians. The incident, though mired in controversy over its origins, became a political and emotional flashpoint. India, driven by domestic outrage and political pressure, chose a bold and aggressive course of action: missile strikes on Pakistani military installations. On May 9, 2025, the Indian military launched direct attacks on airbases including Nur Khan, Murid, and Rafiqui—crossing a red line that had long held back full-scale conflict.

The shockwaves of the assault were immediate and widespread. Civilians were shaken, political leaders were forced into crisis response mode, and Pakistan's military leadership knew that the nation stood at a pivotal moment in its history. The question was no longer if Pakistan would respond—but how. Any retaliation had to reflect national dignity, strategic brilliance, and calculated strength. Rash escalation could mean war; passive restraint could be seen as weakness. The decision made in those critical hours would shape not only the outcome of this conflict but the narrative of Pakistan's standing on the global stage.

What followed was not a chaotic or emotional reaction. It was a carefully planned, highly coordinated military operation named **Bunyan-ul-Marsoos—a Quranic term meaning "a wall of steel."** The name was symbolic, capturing the essence of unity, strength, and divine conviction. This operation wasn't just about returning fire—it was about showing the world what strategic deterrence looks like in the modern era. Pakistan's retaliation was swift, focused, and deeply rooted in faith and discipline. It balanced overwhelming firepower with extraordinary restraint, targeting key Indian military installations and neutralizing advanced defense systems, all while avoiding unnecessary civilian harm.

This book explores the mission behind the headlines. It tells the story not only of missiles and maneuvers but of decisions, doctrines, and dignity. It is a detailed account of how Pakistan's armed forces transformed a moment of vulnerability into one of unmatched national resolve. From the battlefields in the sky to the unseen realm of cyber warfare, and from the coordination rooms of Rawalpindi to the prayer mats of everyday citizens, this was more than a military event—it was a national moment.

Bunyan-ul-Marsoos will be remembered not only as a counterstrike but as a testament to Pakistan's preparedness, precision, and principle. This book seeks to preserve that legacy and offer a deeper understanding of how a nation, under pressure, responded with strength, silence, and thunder.

# Chapter 1
# The Strike That Woke the Nation

The year 2025 will be etched in South Asia's history as a time when a single spark ignited a storm. That spark came in the form of a deadly attack in Pahalgam, a serene town in Indian-administered Kashmir, where dozens of civilians lost their lives in a devastating incident. The immediate blame was directed toward Pakistan, despite a lack of concrete evidence. Within hours, media outrage, political rhetoric, and rising public anger in India pushed the situation beyond diplomacy. It wasn't just an accusation—it was a trigger.

India's leadership, under immense internal pressure, responded with unprecedented military action. On May 9, 2025, missiles were launched at several Pakistani airbases, including Nur Khan, Murid, and Rafiqui. These strikes, bold and direct, shattered a long-standing threshold. They were not covert operations or surgical strikes in contested zones—these were blatant attacks on Pakistan's sovereign military infrastructure. For Pakistan, this was not merely provocation. It was war knocking on the door.

The strikes created immediate confusion and fear among the public. News of the attacks spread like wildfire across social media and news channels. People rushed to stock essential supplies, schools closed, and air raid sirens pierced the night in major cities. Yet amid the anxiety, Pakistan's armed forces moved with swift precision. Emergency protocols were activated. Fighter jets were scrambled. And at the highest levels of command, a decision was taking shape—one that would not only respond to the aggression but would redefine Pakistan's strategic posture.

Thus began the formation of a mission that would come to be known as Bunyan-ul-Marsoos—a retaliation forged with fire, executed with discipline, and remembered as the thunder that awoke a nation under threat.

## The Pahalgam Incident: Catalyst of Conflict

On the misty morning of May 7, 2025, the town of **Pahalgam**, nestled in the heart of Kashmir's tranquil valleys, awoke to a horror it hadn't known in years. Once a symbol of Kashmir's serene beauty and tourist revival, Pahalgam was reduced to chaos in a matter of minutes. A coordinated series of explosions tore through a busy market area and a nearby public gathering spot, killing 48 civilians and injuring more than a hundred others. Among the victims were children, elderly citizens, and tourists. The attack, brutal in its design and shocking in its timing, sent immediate shockwaves across the region.

Indian media outlets erupted with 24-hour coverage, broadcasting horrifying visuals of bloodstained streets and weeping families. Within hours, the Indian government declared the incident an act of terrorism "with undeniable links to Pakistan-based groups," even before any formal investigation could begin. Social media fanned the flames, with hashtags demanding revenge trending nationwide. Public sentiment was inflamed, and political pressure mounted on India's leadership to act decisively.

In the wake of the attack, Indian intelligence agencies hastily compiled a report suggesting that a lesser-known militant group had claimed responsibility—one with alleged historical ties to elements operating out of Pakistan. Despite the absence of verifiable evidence and a lack of formal diplomatic engagement, the narrative was cemented: Pakistan was to blame. Calls for a punitive military response became deafening across Indian political and media circles. The ruling government, facing an upcoming election cycle and a strong nationalist undercurrent, found itself at a crucial decision point.

Pakistan, on the other hand, categorically rejected the allegations. The Ministry of Foreign Affairs issued a formal statement condemning the attack and expressing condolences for the victims, while strongly denying any involvement. Islamabad called for a joint investigation under international oversight, suggesting that premature conclusions were being drawn for political purposes. However, India refused to entertain dialogue or cooperation. The door to diplomacy was not only closed—it was slammed shut.

What made the **Pahalgam incident** particularly dangerous was its **emotional symbolism**. Kashmir has long been a flashpoint between the two nuclear-armed nations. Any act of violence in the region becomes instantly magnified due to its geopolitical sensitivity. This was no exception. For India, the attack was framed as not just another act of terror—but a strike at its sovereignty, unity, and national pride. For Pakistan, the blame was a manufactured narrative used to justify aggression.

The truth of who orchestrated the Pahalgam attack remains shrouded in uncertainty. Some independent analysts raised questions about the speed with which responsibility was assigned. Others highlighted inconsistencies in early reports and the unusual nature of the group said to be behind the attack. Conspiracy theories abounded, suggesting possible internal sabotage or a false flag operation designed to shift focus from domestic challenges in India. But in the absence of conclusive evidence, speculation gave way to action—and action, in this case, took the form of missiles.

On May 9, just two days after the Pahalgam attack, the Indian Air Force launched targeted strikes on three major Pakistani airbases: **Nur Khan**, **Rafiqui**, and **Murid**. These were not disputed border areas or remote militant camps. These were core components of Pakistan's sovereign military infrastructure—located deep inside Pakistani territory. The attacks marked one of the most direct and provocative escalations in recent decades.

India justified the strikes as "preemptive defense," citing its right to neutralize future threats. But to Pakistan, this was nothing short of an act of war—a violation of sovereignty and a reckless gamble with regional peace. For the international community, the development raised immediate alarms, with many fearing that the situation could spiral into a full-scale armed conflict between two nuclear states.

In the aftermath of the Indian strikes, the Pahalgam incident transformed from a tragedy into a **turning point**. What began as a local attack with tragic human cost became the **catalyst of conflict**, reshaping the regional security narrative. It exposed the fragility of deterrence, the danger of assumption-based retaliation, and the growing disconnect between diplomacy and defense in South Asia.

The Pakistani leadership—both military and civilian—now faced a grave challenge. They needed to formulate a response that upheld national dignity, deterred further aggression, and avoided uncalculated escalation. The nation stood at a crossroads where restraint could be seen as weakness and overreaction as recklessness. The answer they forged would soon come in the form of **Operation Bunyan-ul-Marsoos**—a mission that would prove that **Pakistan's silence was not submission, but preparation.**

## Indian Missile Attacks on Pakistani Bases

The tension that followed the Pahalgam incident escalated with frightening speed. On May 9, 2025, in a move that shocked the global community, the Indian Armed Forces launched a series of long-range missile strikes targeting Pakistan's sovereign military installations. The operation, dubbed a "limited retaliatory strike" by Indian officials, was anything but limited in its strategic and symbolic impact. The targets were not militant camps or disputed territories — they were core airbases located deep within Pakistan's recognized borders: PAF Base Nur Khan, PAF Base Murid, and PAF Base Rafiqui.

These bases were not chosen at random. Each held significant strategic value in Pakistan's air defense grid. Nur Khan, formerly Chaklala Airbase, is one of Pakistan's most important military and logistical centers, often used by VVIP aircraft and central command. Murid, located in Punjab, is known for housing key strike and interceptor aircraft. Rafiqui, in Shorkot, is a premier air combat training and deployment base. Together, they form a crucial triad of Pakistan's aerial readiness.

The strikes were sudden and precise. At approximately 4:30 AM local time, Indian missiles — likely variants of the BrahMos and Nirbhay systems — crossed into Pakistani airspace under the radar and struck within seconds. The first wave targeted hangars and runways, aiming to temporarily paralyze air operations. The second wave hit support infrastructure and fuel storage areas. Although the Indian military claimed to avoid civilian casualties, the sheer aggression and brazenness of the attacks left no doubt: this was an act of direct military confrontation.

Initial damage reports were limited due to communication blackouts and rapid lockdowns, but eyewitnesses from areas surrounding the bases reported loud explosions, fireballs lighting the sky, and fighter jets scrambling immediately after the blasts. Emergency services were activated, and residents near the bases were advised to take shelter. Panic spread, especially in Rawalpindi and nearby regions, as civilians feared a full-scale war had just begun.

Pakistan's response in the first hours was measured but firm. The Inter-Services Public Relations (ISPR) acknowledged the attacks, confirmed there were no significant casualties, and stated that Pakistan's defensive systems intercepted several incoming missiles, minimizing the intended damage. However, the gravity of India's actions could not be understated. These strikes were not retaliatory—they were pre-emptive in their planning and designed to send a message of overwhelming force.

India justified its actions as a "counter-terrorism operation" in response to the Pahalgam attack, asserting that intelligence indicated imminent threats emanating from within Pakistan. Yet, there was no concrete evidence presented, no international backing secured, and no attempt made to engage through diplomatic channels. The attack bypassed diplomacy entirely, replacing conversation with confrontation.

The international community reacted with concern and confusion. The United Nations Security Council called an emergency session. China expressed deep alarm over the escalation and called for restraint on both sides. The United States issued a cautious statement urging both nuclear-armed neighbors to de-escalate. Russia called the situation "grave and unprecedented," while several European countries called for investigations into the legality of India's preemptive strikes under international law.

Inside Pakistan, however, the atmosphere was different. Shock gave way to unity. Across the nation, from Lahore to Karachi, the public rallied behind the armed forces. Mosques echoed with prayers, and social media buzzed with messages of solidarity. The national flag flew higher, and a familiar yet somber feeling took hold: Pakistan had been here before—but this time, the nation was ready to respond with purpose, not panic.

Within hours of the strikes, Pakistan's top military leadership convened at GHQ Rawalpindi under the Chairmanship of the Joint Chiefs of Staff. The meeting included the Chief of Army Staff, the Air Chief, the Naval Chief, and key figures from the ISI. There, the decision was made — not in haste, but in clarity: Pakistan would retaliate. But the response would not be blind or emotional; it would be strategic, swift, and surgical.

Thus began the operational planning of what would be named Operation Bunyan-ul-Marsoos — a Quranic term translating to "a wall of steel." The operation was to be Pakistan's message to the world: the country would not be bullied, its sovereignty would not be violated without consequence, and any act of aggression would be met with equal, if not greater, resolve.

The Indian missile attacks were not just military events — they were a declaration. But in declaring war through missiles, India awakened a force that had long prepared for such a moment. Pakistan's silence, as it turned out, was never weakness. It was the quiet before the thunder.

## Civilian Panic and Military Readiness

As the news of missile strikes on Nur Khan, Murid, and Rafiqui Airbases broke across Pakistan on the morning of May 9, 2025, **panic swept the nation like a tidal wave**. The abruptness of the attack, combined with the symbolic weight of the targeted locations, created a nationwide shock. For many civilians, the line between skirmishes and full-scale war had just been crossed. The initial hours were marked by confusion, fear, and a search for answers. Was this the beginning of another war with India? Were more strikes coming? Was this time different?

In Rawalpindi and Islamabad, the proximity to Nur Khan Airbase caused widespread alarm. Loud explosions in the pre-dawn hours startled residents from sleep. Social media lit up with shaky videos of bright flashes in the sky, the hum of jet engines, and plumes of smoke rising in the distance. Emergency sirens were activated in several regions. Radio stations and news channels urged citizens to stay calm, but panic buying of food, water, fuel, and medicine began almost immediately. Pharmacies saw long queues, and grocery stores were emptied within hours.

Parents rushed to schools to pick up children. Offices sent employees home. In Lahore, Karachi, and Peshawar, rumors spread faster than facts—missiles were heading to more cities, fighter jets were downed, airspace was shut. Although not all of it was true, the psychological impact was very real. The mere thought of a sustained Indian attack sent citizens back to the collective trauma of past wars, especially the memories of the 2019 Balakot crisis and the Kargil conflict decades earlier.

In villages near military installations, loudspeakers from mosques and community centers advised people to remain indoors or head to local bunkers where available. In major cities, civil defense protocols were activated, and coordination between provincial governments and federal authorities began in earnest. National television suspended regular programming to deliver continuous coverage. Religious scholars appeared on air, offering spiritual reassurance, while political analysts debated the unfolding crisis and speculated on the government's response.

Yet amid this civilian panic, a contrasting atmosphere existed within the corridors of power and military command. While the public grappled with uncertainty, **Pakistan's armed forces moved with clarity and resolve**. Within minutes of the first strike, emergency contingency protocols were enacted. All branches of the military were placed on high alert. Airbases across the country were secured. Radar systems and early-warning surveillance mechanisms went into overdrive. High-value assets, including fighter jets, command aircraft, and critical infrastructure, were repositioned or camouflaged to reduce vulnerability to follow-up attacks.

The **Pakistan Air Force (PAF)**, renowned for its agility and discipline, was the first to respond. Within minutes, **combat air** patrols (CAPs) were launched across multiple sectors. JF-17 Thunder and F-16 squadrons took to the skies to secure airspace and ensure no further violations. The PAF's quick response validated years of joint training and simulation drills. Pilots were already stationed on rotation due to heightened regional tensions, and runway readiness drills had been intensified in recent weeks. Every second was accounted for.

The **Army Strategic Forces Command** was also placed on standby, a move not made lightly. While Pakistan did not intend to escalate to strategic warfare, readiness was essential to deter further aggression. At sea, the **Pakistan Navy** activated key maritime defense zones, especially around the Arabian Sea, where naval installations could be vulnerable to surprise strikes or submarine incursions.

Behind the scenes, **the Inter-Services Intelligence (ISI) and Military Intelligence (MI)** began rapidly compiling threat assessments and intercepting communications. Their immediate goal was to determine if India intended this as a one-off strike or the beginning of a broader offensive. Diplomatically, the Foreign Office briefed key embassies and alerted Pakistan's allies, particularly China, Turkey, and Saudi Arabia, about the unprovoked act of aggression. The government also initiated backchannel communication with global powers to prevent premature escalation.

One of the defining features of Pakistan's readiness was its **strategic restraint under fire**. Instead of rushing into a counterattack or issuing reactionary statements, the leadership—both military and civilian—chose to assess, organize, and prepare. This restraint was not weakness, but the hallmark of a mature military doctrine. It allowed time to verify facts, calculate the enemy's intentions, and craft a response that would be effective, lawful, and overwhelming—when the time came.

By nightfall on May 9, the panic among civilians had begun to give way to resilience. Citizens lit candles in solidarity, mosques filled with worshippers praying for peace, and Pakistani flags appeared on balconies and storefronts. Fear turned into unity, confusion into confidence. The nation now looked toward GHQ, toward the skies, and toward the silence before thunder—with a collective, unspoken message: **Strike with purpose. Strike with pride.**

The stage was now set for **Operation Bunyan-ul-Marsoos**—not just a military operation, but a message engraved in steel.

# Chapter 2
# Enter Bunyan-ul-Marsoos

In the immediate aftermath of the Indian missile strikes, Pakistan stood at a defining crossroads. The nation had been violated—its airspace breached, its bases targeted—but it had not been broken. The military leadership, backed by the civilian government and unified public sentiment, now faced the crucial decision of how and when to respond. This response could not be hasty, nor could it be weak. It had to be exact, deliberate, and historic.

It was during this pivotal moment that Pakistan's armed forces unveiled the name of the counteroffensive: **Operation Bunyan-ul-Marsoos**. The name was not chosen lightly. Derived from **Surah As-Saff, verse 4** of the Holy Qur'an, the phrase translates to *"a solidly constructed wall"*—a metaphor for unshakable strength, unity, and divine purpose. The operation was to reflect Pakistan's military capability, national discipline, and unwavering faith.

Bunyan-ul-Marsoos was more than a name—it was a doctrine. It was the embodiment of a measured response that would demonstrate precision without provocation, resolve without recklessness. The mission would be multi-dimensional, involving air superiority, intelligence operations, cyber capabilities, and psychological warfare. But above all, it would be grounded in the belief that Pakistan's strength lies not only in its arsenal, but in its unity and moral clarity.

This chapter delves into the **significance of the operation's name**, the **delicate process of forming a coordinated response**, and the **role of faith as a guiding force** in Pakistan's strategic decision-making. It marks the beginning of a campaign that would redefine deterrence in the region—and remind the world that silence, when backed by conviction, can roar louder than war itself.

## Naming the Mission: Meaning and Significance

When the time came for Pakistan to respond to the Indian missile attacks on its airbases, the decision-makers within the highest echelons of the military knew that the retaliation had to be more than just military—it had to be moral, symbolic, and message-driven. Every aspect of the operation needed to reflect not just Pakistan's military preparedness but also its national values and spiritual identity. This philosophy crystallized in the name chosen for the mission: Bunyan-ul-Marsoos.

Taken from **Surah As-Saff (61:4)** in the Holy Qur'an, the term *Bunyan-ul-Marsoos* translates to **"a wall of steel"** or **"a solidly constructed wall."** The full verse praises those who fight in the cause of truth as if they are "a solid wall," indicating both unity and divine support in righteous struggle. The name was more than poetic—it was purposeful. It conveyed to both domestic and international audiences that Pakistan's response was rooted in defense, not aggression; in unity, not division; and above all, in the unwavering belief that truth and justice stand strongest when bound together like a wall of steel.

The phrase had never been used for a military operation in Pakistan's history. Its introduction marked a **new chapter** in strategic doctrine—one where the spiritual and the tactical intertwined. In a time when military actions are often reduced to acronyms and impersonal codenames, Bunyan-ul-Marsoos stood out. It carried **philosophical depth**, evoked religious resonance, and encapsulated the tone Pakistan wished to set: resolute, righteous, and restrained.

The selection of the name followed intense deliberation among senior military officials, intelligence heads, and strategic planners. The leadership was fully aware that the name would echo beyond briefing rooms—it would be on headlines, diplomatic reports, and eventually, in the annals of history. Thus, it had to be more than a label; it had to encapsulate the **entire spirit of the operation**. After reviewing several options, Bunyan-ul-Marsoos was chosen unanimously—not only for its Quranic roots but for the psychological strength it projected.

This was a war not just of weapons but of narratives. India had quickly labeled its own strikes as "preemptive," designed to dismantle imminent threats. In doing so, it sought to frame Pakistan as the aggressor and itself as a reluctant warrior. Pakistan needed to reclaim the narrative, and the operation's name would be the first weapon in that counter-narrative. By invoking a divine metaphor, Pakistan signaled that its actions were defensive, deliberate, and dignified—not impulsive or expansionist.

Domestically, the name stirred **immense pride and emotional unity**. Citizens embraced it as a powerful reminder of faith in adversity. The name was widely shared across social media platforms, written on placards at public rallies, and quoted in Friday sermons. Analysts praised the decision for aligning military strength with national spirituality. For many, it recalled the ethos of past leaders who spoke of "jihad with purpose" and "defense with dignity"—but with a modernized, controlled execution in the form of Bunyan-ul-Marsoos.

Internationally, the name prompted curiosity and cautious admiration. Foreign analysts unfamiliar with the Quranic reference initially struggled to understand its implications. But soon, the phrase began to appear in think tank papers, diplomatic briefings, and media coverage. It became clear that this was no impulsive revenge mission. Pakistan had crafted a message embedded with historical, cultural, and religious depth—aimed as much at the world as it was at its adversary.

The symbolic choice of Bunyan-ul-Marsoos also aligned closely with Pakistan's **internal doctrine of strategic restraint**. Unlike other nations that might react with overwhelming force and indiscriminate retaliation, Pakistan's leadership chose a path that combined precision with principle. The name reflected this balance: the strength of steel paired with the integrity of a cause. It allowed Pakistan to demonstrate power without boasting, capability without chaos.

In essence, the naming of Operation Bunyan-ul-Marsoos served three vital purposes: **it united the nation, reframed the narrative**, and **projected a morally grounded deterrent**. It was not merely about responding to India's provocations; it was about doing so in a way that aligned with Pakistan's identity as a Muslim-majority nation committed to justice, faith, and sovereignty.

As the operation unfolded and Pakistani forces executed their meticulously planned retaliatory strikes, the name **Bunyan-ul-Marsoos** gained weight. It transformed from a strategic phrase into a national symbol—one that echoed in the roar of fighter jets, the calculated cyber offensives, and the resilient silence of a nation that refused to be broken.

In the end, **the name was not just heard—it was felt**, in the hearts of the citizens, the confidence of the soldiers, and the caution of the world. Pakistan had spoken, not just with firepower, but with meaning.

## Formation of a Unified Response Strategy

As the dust settled from the Indian missile strikes, Pakistan's leadership faced a critical and unprecedented challenge—how to respond. The pressure was immense. The public was watching, the military was mobilizing, and the international community was measuring every move. Any misstep could either escalate the conflict beyond control or diminish Pakistan's credibility. In that fragile moment, what unfolded was a masterclass in unified strategic coordination, involving all branches of the armed forces, intelligence agencies, and the civilian leadership.

The process began within hours of the strikes. A high-level emergency meeting was called at the General Headquarters (GHQ) in Rawalpindi, chaired by the Chief of Army Staff (COAS) and attended by the Air Chief Marshal, the Naval Chief, the Director-General of ISI, the National Security Advisor, and senior representatives from the Prime Minister's Office. The objective was clear: to assess the scale of damage, determine India's intention, and craft a calculated response that would restore deterrence without triggering full-scale war.

Unlike past regional skirmishes that were reactive in nature, the decision-making this time was methodical and multidimensional. The response would be coordinated across land, air, cyber, and diplomatic fronts, with an emphasis on strategic timing, intelligence-backed targeting, and complete inter-service cooperation.

The Pakistan Air Force (PAF) took the lead in offensive planning. Within 12 hours, target analysis teams, surveillance units, and flight command units had compiled a prioritized list of Indian military sites, logistics hubs, and key command-and-control centers. Strikes had to be precise—not symbolic—so as to demonstrate capability without opening the door to uncontrolled escalation. Satellite data, drone footage, and HUMINT (human intelligence) were combined in real time to develop strike packages that would inflict tactical damage and send a powerful message of resolve.

The Pakistan Army focused on readiness across the Line of Control (LoC) and Eastern borders. Troops were repositioned, defensive perimeters were reinforced, and heavy artillery units were put on alert. However, unlike previous conflicts, the Army's role was primarily strategic containment—ensuring that ground-based incursions or escalations would be rapidly neutralized, but without initiating unnecessary aggression.

Simultaneously, the Pakistan Navy deployed its assets to monitor the maritime situation in the Arabian Sea, particularly around Indian naval corridors. Naval intelligence tracked submarine movements and mobilized Pakistan's naval aviation fleet for potential reconnaissance operations. The Navy's role was to serve as a deterrent in case the conflict expanded to the sea, ensuring readiness without provocation.

Perhaps the most critical element in the unified strategy was the role played by intelligence agencies, led by the Inter-Services Intelligence (ISI). Tasked with early warning, target verification, and psychological operations, the ISI worked closely with military planners to verify intelligence before any operation was greenlit. More importantly, they monitored Indian communications and internal political discourse, ensuring that Pakistan stayed ahead of India's next possible move.

A major part of the strategy was also cyber defense and offense. Pakistan's cyber command, operating under the Strategic Plans Division, launched containment operations to shield national infrastructure from digital sabotage while simultaneously launching precision cyber intrusions into Indian military networks. This two-way cyber strategy gave Pakistan an edge in real-time information warfare, allowing it to monitor Indian command channels and feed false signals where necessary.

While the military apparatus was in high gear, the civilian leadership played a key strategic role in ensuring international diplomacy and domestic calm. The Prime Minister held private consultations with key cabinet members, while the Foreign Ministry initiated contact with world powers including China, Turkey, and Saudi Arabia. Special envoys were dispatched to the United Nations and the Organization of Islamic Cooperation (OIC), presenting a detailed case of unprovoked aggression and Pakistan's right to defend its sovereignty.

One of the most remarkable aspects of this phase was the seamless coordination between civilian and military leadership—a relationship that has often been marked by tension in Pakistan's past. This time, unity prevailed. The Prime Minister gave full operational autonomy to the military while retaining strategic oversight and control over diplomatic engagement. National television was carefully used to communicate with the public—

assuring strength, explaining restraint, and preparing the nation for what was to come.

By the evening of May 10, the entire operation was finalized. It was not just a counterstrike—it was a carefully choreographed military and psychological campaign, designed to reestablish deterrence, defend honor, and control escalation. Operation Bunyan-ul-Marsoos had now moved from conception to execution.

The formation of this unified response strategy proved that modern warfare is not just about weapons—it's about synchronization. Land, air, sea, cyber, intelligence, and diplomacy — every piece of Pakistan's national power apparatus moved in harmony. The enemy had launched a calculated strike. Pakistan's answer would be measured, multi-domain, and magnificent.

## Faith as a Foundation for Action

As Operation Bunyan-ul-Marsoos moved from planning to execution, one force stood silently at the core of Pakistan's response — **faith**. It was not just an ideological backdrop or a rhetorical tool; it was the **central pillar** guiding decisions, actions, and discipline. In the face of external aggression and internal anxiety, faith provided clarity, resolve, and unity — elements that proved just as vital as aircraft, missiles, or intelligence networks.

Pakistan, a nation born in the name of Islam, has always carried its spiritual identity into moments of great national testing. The Quranic name "Bunyan-ul-Marsoos" — *a wall of steel* — was not just a military codename; it was a direct invocation of divine principle. Taken from **Surah As-Saff (61:4)**, the verse describes believers who fight "in the cause of Allah, as if they were a solid wall." This verse was chosen with intentional symbolism. The leadership wanted the entire operation to reflect discipline, sacrifice, and unity not just in physical terms, but in spiritual alignment.

This faith-inspired framework had a practical impact on all levels of the military structure. From the top brass at GHQ to pilots preparing for critical airstrikes, there was a shared conviction that **this was not just a military response—it was a defense of truth and sovereignty**. Soldiers and airmen didn't merely follow orders; they carried out their duties with a sense of moral responsibility and spiritual purpose. It wasn't just about avenging a strike — it was about fulfilling a duty to defend the homeland in accordance with deeply rooted principles.

Mosques within military installations were filled in the days leading up to the operation. Senior officers, troops, and civilian defense staff could be seen offering prayers, reading the Quran, and seeking guidance. There was no need to command such acts — they arose organically, as part of a culture where faith and duty are intimately intertwined. Friday sermons across the country echoed the Quranic verse, and scholars reminded citizens that **jihad**, in this context, was not about conquest—it was about **defending the oppressed, upholding justice, and preserving peace**.

For many of the pilots who participated in the planned retaliatory strikes, faith served as their armor. One PAF officer, whose story was later shared anonymously in national media, was quoted saying, *"When I took off, I was prepared to strike with accuracy. But when I returned, I felt as if I had fulfilled a responsibility far greater than myself. I did not fly just as a soldier, but as a servant of truth."* This sentiment was not isolated—it was echoed in countless briefings, barracks, and mess halls.

Faith also played a crucial role in managing public sentiment. In the days of confusion and panic following the Indian attacks, religious leaders helped **anchor the nation's emotions**. Rather than inflaming tensions, most Islamic scholars and clerics called for patience, prayer, and trust in Pakistan's leadership. Their messages were aligned with the military's posture of **measured retaliation** and reinforced the idea that the nation would not act out of revenge, but from a place of principled strength.

Even in the realm of **international diplomacy**, faith-based messaging served a subtle yet powerful purpose. Pakistan's Foreign Office deliberately referenced Quranic ethics in its briefings to OIC member states, emphasizing that Pakistan had been attacked without provocation and was responding with dignity and self-restraint — values rooted in Islamic justice. This language resonated with allies like Turkey, Saudi Arabia, and Malaysia, who expressed solidarity not just politically, but culturally and spiritually.

Internally, faith helped create a **shared language** between the military, government, and people. Where complex strategic language might distance the average citizen from understanding national security decisions, the moral clarity of Quranic guidance offered connection and coherence. Citizens understood that Pakistan was not just reacting — it was standing firm, as commanded, like a wall of steel against falsehood and aggression.

It is important to note that this spiritual foundation did not compromise professional military standards. On the contrary, it **enhanced discipline**. Faith became a motivating force that demanded not only courage but precision, not only pride but humility. The belief that accountability was not just to commanders, but ultimately to Allah, instilled a level of seriousness and focus that elevated operational performance.

In essence, **faith was the invisible force that held the visible strategy together**. It was the heartbeat of Operation Bunyan-ul-Marsoos — steady, strong, and unshakable. In a world increasingly driven by technology and geopolitics, Pakistan reminded its enemies and allies alike that the soul of a nation still matters. Its spiritual spine, forged in the fires of history and nourished by belief, proved to be as vital as any jet engine or radar.

Operation Bunyan-ul-Marsoos was not just an answer to an attack — it was a declaration that **Pakistan's strength lies not only in steel, but in spirit**.

# Chapter 3
# Strategic Calculations

Following the Indian missile strikes, Pakistan found itself on the edge of a moment that could alter the trajectory of South Asian security for decades to come. The initial instinct in such situations is often emotional: strike back hard, fast, and without hesitation. But in a nuclear-armed region where one wrong move could trigger a catastrophic chain reaction, Pakistan's leadership chose a different path — a path defined by **discipline, strategy, and calibrated force**.

This chapter explores the intricate thought process behind Pakistan's military response. The stakes were high: the world was watching, allies were weighing in quietly, and domestic expectations were rising rapidly. The challenge was not whether to retaliate — that decision was inevitable — but **how** to retaliate in a way that preserved national dignity, restored deterrence, and avoided uncontrolled escalation.

The corridors of **GHQ Rawalpindi** and the **Pakistan Air Force Command** became the central hubs of intense deliberation. Top military planners, intelligence chiefs, and strategic advisors gathered in war rooms to study scenarios, assess risks, and craft a response that would be both **surgical and symbolic**. Retaliation would come, but not at the cost of strategic misjudgment.

This chapter delves into the **balance between restraint and resolve**, the **briefings that defined Pakistan's precision**, and the **seamless coordination** between the Army, Air Force, and intelligence agencies that laid the foundation for Operation Bunyan-ul-Marsoos. It was a time when calculated decisions carried more power than raw fire — a moment when steel had to be sharpened by wisdom.

## Balancing Retaliation with Restraint

Retaliation in the face of military aggression is not just expected — it is often demanded. When a nation's sovereignty is violated, the pressure to respond swiftly and forcefully can be overwhelming. But in the modern world, especially in a region like South Asia where two nuclear-armed powers stand in opposition, military decisions must be guided not by emotion but by strategic calculation. This was the central dilemma facing Pakistan's leadership in the hours after the Indian missile attacks: how to strike back with strength and clarity, without tipping the region into chaos.

The attacks on Nur Khan, Murid, and Rafiqui Airbases were unprecedented in their directness and danger. They marked a clear escalation, one that crossed long-standing red lines. Public sentiment in Pakistan surged with righteous anger. Social media echoed with calls for revenge, and many civilians feared that all-out war was imminent. In such an atmosphere, history has often shown that nations make hasty decisions that lead to long-term consequences.

But Pakistan's response defied the usual script. Instead of reacting impulsively, the country's military and civilian leadership chose a path of measured retaliation, grounded in clarity, confidence, and restraint. This decision was not a sign of weakness

— it was the hallmark of mature strategic thinking. Pakistan was not looking to start a war, but it was determined to restore deterrence and reaffirm that its sovereignty was not negotiable.

The initial hours were spent gathering intelligence, confirming the scale of damage, and analyzing India's motives. Was the strike intended as a one-time political gesture, or was it the beginning of a broader military campaign? Would India escalate if Pakistan responded proportionally? How would the international community perceive Pakistan's next move? These questions dominated the early deliberations within the war rooms of GHQ Rawalpindi and the Air Force's Strategic Command.

Key military planners understood that while the need for response was urgent, the **method of response** mattered more. Pakistan had the capability to launch large-scale strikes across multiple Indian targets within hours. However, such a move would invite immediate escalation and potentially draw both countries into a sustained conflict — one neither side could afford. The challenge was to find a response that was **strong enough to send a message**, yet **limited enough to contain escalation**.

This led to the birth of a retaliatory framework guided by three principles: **precision, proportionality, and perception**.

**Precision** meant that targets would be selected based on military value, not symbolic optics alone. Strikes would focus on Indian military infrastructure, logistics hubs, and weapons storage facilities — avoiding civilian areas or overly provocative locations. The goal was to degrade capability without triggering emotional outrage that could spiral into wider conflict.

**Proportionality** ensured that the scale and intensity of Pakistan's response matched India's level of aggression. The idea was to create a strategic equilibrium: Pakistan would not respond disproportionately, but it would not respond weakly either. This careful calibration would preserve credibility while denying India any justification for further escalation.

**Perception** referred to how the response would be viewed domestically, regionally, and internationally. Within Pakistan, the response had to satisfy public expectations and demonstrate strength. Regionally, it had to signal deterrence to India and other potential adversaries. Internationally, it had to be seen as a **legitimate act of self-defense** rather than the ignition of war. Pakistan's leadership was well aware that global opinion, especially from powers like China, the US, Russia, and Gulf states, would play a role in shaping the aftermath.

The ultimate result of this balancing act was Operation Bunyan-ul-Marsoos — a military campaign rooted in faith, backed by intelligence, and executed with discipline. It was designed to **send shockwaves through Indian military command**, without pushing South Asia over the brink.

This approach was widely praised, even by neutral observers. International analysts noted the contrast between India's unilateral escalation and Pakistan's methodical response. While India rushed into a strike with questionable justification, Pakistan took the time to assess, prepare, and respond with clarity and control. In doing so, it **reclaimed the moral and strategic high ground**.

At its core, the decision to balance retaliation with restraint showed that **power is not only about what you can destroy, but what you choose to protect**. Pakistan demonstrated that strength is not measured by volume of firepower alone, but by the wisdom to use it responsibly.

In an age where geopolitics is increasingly driven by instant reactions and short-term optics, Pakistan's response stood as a reminder that **restraint is not retreat — it is leadership**. And through that leadership, Pakistan not only defended its skies, but also its reputation, its dignity, and the fragile peace of an entire region.

## Briefings at GHQ and Air Force Command

In the immediate aftermath of the Indian missile strikes on May 9, 2025, the **General Headquarters (GHQ) in Rawalpindi** and the **Pakistan Air Force (PAF) Command** transformed into nerve centers of intense strategic deliberation. The corridors of both institutions, usually buzzing with routine military activity, now echoed with urgency, purpose, and an unspoken gravity. Decisions made in these rooms would not only shape Pakistan's response but potentially define the geopolitical stability of the entire region.

The first high-level briefing was convened at GHQ within hours of the strikes. It was chaired by the **Chief of Army Staff (COAS)** and attended by the **Air Chief Marshal, Naval Chief, Director-General of Inter-Services Intelligence (ISI)**, senior officers from the Joint Chiefs of Staff Committee, and strategic advisors from the Prime Minister's Office. The atmosphere was tense but focused. Everyone present understood the magnitude of the moment. This was not a drill. This was not a border skirmish. This was **an open act of war** that required a measured but resolute response.

The meeting began with detailed **situation reports (SITREPs)** from all affected airbases. Officers from Nur Khan, Murid, and Rafiqui briefed the leadership on the extent of damage, loss of infrastructure, operational readiness, and casualty counts. Thanks to

Pakistan's early-warning systems and preparedness drills, major assets had been moved in time, resulting in limited material damage and no significant loss of life. However, the symbolism of the attack was significant. India had not struck proxies or border posts — it had **targeted the core of Pakistan's sovereign air defense system**.

Following the SITREPs, intelligence briefings were presented by the ISI and Military Intelligence (MI). Surveillance drones, satellite imagery, and intercepted communications provided a fuller picture of the situation on the Indian side. The briefings revealed that India had not mobilized for a full-scale war, but had instead executed a carefully planned limited strike — likely with the intention of **sending a political message** rather than starting an all-out conflict. This insight was critical. It suggested that while India had escalated the situation, it might not seek further confrontation unless provoked beyond a threshold.

At **Air Headquarters Islamabad**, the Air Chief Marshal led a parallel session focusing specifically on air capabilities, retaliation options, and readiness levels. Here, **strike planning teams** presented various operational blueprints, ranging from minimal symbolic strikes to more aggressive multi-front assaults. Each option came with risk assessments, escalation projections, and estimated timeframes for execution.

What stood out in these briefings was the **depth of preparedness**. For months, if not years, Pakistan's military leadership had anticipated such a scenario. Regular joint exercises, inter-service war games, and crisis simulations had prepared commanders to deal with sudden aggression. Now, those scenarios had come to life — and the military's ability to shift from simulation to real-world execution was seamless.

The briefings also focused on **target selection**. Intelligence had already provided a shortlist of high-value Indian targets, including ammunition depots, logistics hubs, air force installations, and missile storage sites. These were carefully reviewed for strategic impact, collateral risk, and proximity to civilian infrastructure. The priority was clear: **retaliate in a way that disabled capability, not provoked public outrage**.

As the sessions advanced, the coordination between GHQ and Air Headquarters became more integrated. Secure communication lines allowed real-time sharing of data, plans, and updates. Representatives from the **Strategic Plans Division** and **Cyber Command** were also involved, ensuring that digital warfare options were synchronized with kinetic operations. In parallel, legal and diplomatic advisors briefed leadership on international law parameters to ensure that Pakistan's response remained **within the bounds of self-defense under Article 51 of the UN Charter.**

By the end of the second day, the command structures had reached a decision. The retaliation would come in the form of **Operation Bunyan-ul-Marsoos** — a term rooted in Quranic metaphor but backed by real-time precision, technological sophistication, and unified command. The final briefings laid out execution timelines, fallback strategies, counter-escalation plans, and communication protocols for both domestic and global stakeholders.

One of the key outcomes of these briefings was the **reinforcement of civilian-military harmony**. Throughout the process, the Prime Minister and the National Security Council were kept fully informed, and all strategic decisions were made with collective agreement. This level of transparency and cooperation was instrumental in ensuring **national coherence** during a period of high tension.

Ultimately, the briefings at GHQ and Air Force Command served as the intellectual engine behind Pakistan's response. They were not merely updates — they were the **frameworks of resolve**, blending real-time intelligence, military experience, and national vision. They proved that when faced with deliberate provocation, Pakistan would not just react — it would **respond with precision, professionalism, and purpose**.

## Coordination Between Army, Air Force, and Intelligence

In the modern landscape of warfare, no successful military operation is executed by a single branch of the armed forces in isolation. Victory lies in synergy — a seamless integration of ground, air, sea, and intelligence assets working in unified precision. Operation Bunyan-ul-Marsoos became a **textbook case of tri-service coordination**, with the Pakistan Army, Air Force, and intelligence agencies executing a retaliatory response that was not only swift and calculated, but also deeply synchronized.

The Indian missile strikes on Nur Khan, Murid, and Rafiqui airbases triggered a nationwide state of alert. Yet within the framework of alarm and urgency, Pakistan's military leadership responded with calm, order, and unified purpose. GHQ Rawalpindi quickly became the central coordination hub, where strategic planners from all branches converged to develop an operational framework that could deliver retaliation without uncontrolled escalation.

The **Pakistan Air Force (PAF)**, by nature of the initial attack, took tactical lead in the mission. Retaliatory strikes would be conducted through air operations, and the burden of planning, targeting, and execution rested primarily on the Air Force. However, the effectiveness of these air missions relied heavily on the support of ground-based military assets and real-time intelligence from national security agencies.

From the onset, the **Pakistan Army** played a crucial role in securing forward and border-based assets, positioning air defense systems, and maintaining heightened readiness along the Line of Control (LoC) and Eastern border. Ground-based radar systems, air-defense missile batteries, and anti-aircraft artillery were repositioned in coordination with air surveillance patterns to create a layered shield around critical infrastructure. The Army's Corps of Signals provided secure communication links between various operational units, while field engineers fortified temporary command posts for mobility and responsiveness.

Simultaneously, **intelligence coordination** became the backbone of the entire operation. The **Inter-Services Intelligence (ISI)**, in tandem with **Military Intelligence (MI)** and **Air Intelligence**, operated around the clock to feed real-time data into the operational command centers. Surveillance drones monitored enemy troop movement, strategic radar tracked Indian aircraft positioning, and electronic signals intelligence intercepted communications that indicated India's next possible moves.

This **data-driven collaboration** enabled the Air Force to refine its target lists. Proposed strike zones were vetted multiple times, not only for military value but for broader implications — including escalation risk, international perception, and potential civilian proximity. It was here that the intelligence agencies proved their worth, offering not just battlefield insight but geopolitical context, allowing the military to act with surgical accuracy.

Regular **Joint Coordination Briefings** were held multiple times a day. These briefings included representatives from the COAS's office, Air Headquarters, ISI's strategic operations cell, and Naval Intelligence liaisons. While the Navy remained largely on defensive posture during this operation, it contributed by securing maritime borders and monitoring potential naval deployments from the Indian side.

One of the most critical aspects of coordination was the **real-time integration of aerial missions with intelligence validation**. Air Force strike teams would not take off until clearance had been confirmed by ISI analysts who had verified enemy movement in the target zone. This ensured that each strike was not only relevant, but also current. The margin of error was razor-thin — and Pakistan's forces operated within that margin with extraordinary precision.

At the same time, the Army's logistical support helped move equipment, launch decoys, and prepare alternative airstrips for emergency landings. Commandos from Special Services Group (SSG) were stationed at key airbases as quick reaction forces in case of sabotage or internal breach. These units were in constant communication with Air Force security regiments and military police to safeguard personnel and installations.

Cyber defense and digital coordination were also critical. Military cyber units monitored Indian news outlets, social media trends, and open-source chatter to assess public and diplomatic reaction to Pakistan's posture. They also ensured that misinformation campaigns, whether internal or cross-border, were rapidly countered. This multi-domain coordination ensured not only military success but control over the **information war**.

Perhaps the most remarkable feature of this operation was the **absence of friction between the services**. Historically, even the best militaries in the world struggle with inter-service rivalry or procedural delays during joint operations. But during Operation Bunyan-ul-Marsoos, Pakistan's forces demonstrated a rare degree of operational unity. Decisions flowed smoothly. Intelligence was shared rapidly. Commanders trusted each other's assessments and acted without hesitation.

This seamless coordination created a combat rhythm that would define the success of the operation. Each branch of the armed forces operated like a vital organ in a single, functioning body — different roles, but one mission: **to deliver a response that restored balance, protected sovereignty, and reaffirmed deterrence**.

Operation Bunyan-ul-Marsoos became a model for how national defense should function in the 21st century — a fusion of **air power, ground stability, intelligence supremacy, and institutional unity**. It was not just a mission. It was a message — and it was delivered together.

# Chapter 4
# Precision in the Sky

With the planning phase of Operation Bunyan-ul-Marsoos complete, Pakistan now stood at the edge of execution. The world was watching with bated breath, allies were quietly supportive, and adversaries were uncertain. It was time for action — not broad, blunt retaliation, but a demonstration of calibrated airpower driven by intelligence, restraint, and precision.

This chapter explores the pivotal moment when the Pakistan Air Force (PAF) took center stage. Following days of round-the-clock briefings, intelligence analysis, and inter-service coordination, the time had come to deliver a response that would reaffirm Pakistan's air dominance and strategic capability. But this was not a campaign of vengeance — it was a deliberate act of military discipline aimed at restoring deterrence and sending an unmistakable message: Pakistan would never be caught off guard again.

At the heart of this operation lay three foundational elements: target selection rooted in tactical value rather than emotional symbolism, uninterrupted drone surveillance and reconnaissance flights to validate enemy movements, and the synchronization of strike squadrons for flawless air operations. This was warfare governed by logic, not impulse; by calculated risk, not raw aggression.

The air strikes that followed would be remembered not for their noise, but for their surgical silence — swift, clean, and devastatingly effective. Every sortie, every maneuver, every payload carried with it not just explosive potential, but national resolve.

In this chapter, we go inside the skies where the true response unfolded — not in speeches, not in headlines, but in the roar of afterburners and the precision of guided payloads. This is the story of how Pakistan struck back — not just with steel, but with strategy.

## Target Selection: Beyond Symbolism

One of the most critical phases of Operation Bunyan-ul-Marsoos was the selection of targets. This was not merely about choosing sites to destroy — it was about crafting a message with precision. Pakistan's response had to reflect strength without recklessness, control without compromise. The leadership understood that true deterrence lay not in the volume of firepower, but in its deliberate and focused application. Every target chosen had to serve a strategic, operational, and psychological purpose.

In the early days following India's missile attack, dozens of potential targets were identified across Northern and Central India. These included airbases, missile storage facilities, logistics hubs, radar installations, fuel depots, ammunition dumps, and command-and-control centers. However, the challenge wasn't in locating targets — it was in prioritizing them for maximum impact with minimal escalation.

Pakistan's Air Intelligence, working in close collaboration with ISI and satellite surveillance teams, categorized targets into three tiers. Tier 1 included high-value military installations directly involved in recent aggression — such as Pathankot Airbase, Adampur Airbase, and missile storage units in Beas and Nagrota. These were operationally active sites that supported offensive capability and posed a continuing threat. Tier 2 included radar and surveillance stations that could limit Pakistan's future air movement. Tier 3 targets included logistics and fuel depots that, while not immediately dangerous, could impair India's long-term readiness.

What made Pakistan's approach unique was its avoidance of symbolic or civilian targets. Unlike in some past conflicts where strategic restraint gave way to emotionally driven responses, Bunyan-ul-Marsoos was guided by principle. The aim was not to create headlines by striking monuments or symbolic cities — the aim was to create operational paralysis. India would be left guessing what would be hit next, unsure of its own vulnerabilities, and acutely aware that Pakistan had struck with surgical accuracy.

Each shortlisted target was assessed under three primary filters:

1. **Military Value**: Could the destruction of this site impair India's operational ability or restrict its aggression in the coming weeks?

2. **Escalation Control**: Would hitting this site be seen as legitimate under international law, or could it be interpreted as an unjustified escalation?

3. **Collateral Minimization**: Could the strike be executed without endangering civilian lives or property in the vicinity?

The decision to strike Pathankot and Adampur airbases was not accidental. These bases had long played a key role in Indian air operations against Pakistan and were linked to earlier mobilizations. Destroying fuel storage, disabling aircraft shelters, and targeting hardened shelters there had both tactical and symbolic value — they reminded India that no base is untouchable.

Striking BrahMos missile storage facilities in Beas and Nagrota served a dual purpose. Tactically, it reduced the risk of a second Indian strike using the subsonic cruise missile system. Psychologically, it sent a message that even India's prized assets could be neutralized. These locations were selected based on months of intelligence gathering, satellite imagery, and signal intercepts, with Pakistani planners fully aware of the risks involved — but also confident in the strategic gain.

Importantly, the PAF deliberately avoided high-density urban centers or purely symbolic targets. There were no strikes on political buildings, civilian airports, or historical landmarks. This disciplined targeting decision impressed many international observers, who saw it as evidence of Pakistan's mature strategic doctrine. It wasn't just about hitting back — it was about doing so within the moral and legal framework of self-defense.

This precision-centric targeting model also served to keep the international community on Pakistan's side. While the Indian media portrayed Pakistan as a reckless actor, global military analysts and foreign governments acknowledged the professionalism of its response. By focusing exclusively on military targets, Pakistan effectively framed its counterstrike as a justified, proportionate act of defense under Article 51 of the UN Charter.

Behind every selected target, there was also a message. To the Indian military, it said: Your offensive will be met with force. To the Indian government, it said: You have crossed a line, and now face consequences. To the Pakistani people, it said: You are defended by skill, not by chaos. And to the world, it said: We can respond without losing control.

In the end, target selection in Operation Bunyan-ul-Marsoos was not just about destruction — it was about demonstrating resolve through restraint, power through precision, and sovereignty through strategy. It showed that in modern warfare, where public perception and legal justification are as important as battlefield success, Pakistan had evolved — and its response would reflect that evolution.

## Drone Surveillance and Recon Flights

In the age of modern warfare, intelligence is no longer gathered by men in the field alone — it is captured from the sky, in real time, by unmanned aerial vehicles (UAVs) and high-altitude reconnaissance systems. During Operation Bunyan-ul-Marsoos, Pakistan's ability to monitor, verify, and assess enemy movement relied heavily on a multi-layered surveillance strategy, with drones and recon flights at its core. This technological edge gave the Pakistan Air Force (PAF) and military command a decisive advantage in choosing their targets, confirming enemy vulnerabilities, and executing coordinated air strikes with surgical accuracy.

From the moment India launched missile attacks on Pakistani airbases, the PAF initiated a 24/7 drone surveillance grid over sensitive sectors, including the Line of Control (LoC), border regions, and known Indian military corridors. The use of advanced tactical drones—such as the Shahpar-II, Burraq, and several Chinese-origin reconnaissance UAVs—created a live intelligence network feeding real-time visuals and telemetry to command centers in Islamabad, Rawalpindi, and PAF Base Mushaf.

The first objective of these drone flights was damage assessment. UAVs were dispatched over the targeted airbases—Nur Khan, Rafiqui, and Murid—to survey infrastructure impact, ensure the safety of grounded aircraft, and verify runway integrity. Simultaneously, additional drones were directed toward Indian airfields to monitor any signs of further escalation or mobilization. These missions were carried out at varying altitudes to avoid radar detection, with some drones flying at low altitudes using terrain-masking techniques and others hovering at high altitude for wide-area scanning.

But drones weren't just used for surveillance—they were used to validate targets and confirm strike readiness. Pakistani intelligence agencies had compiled a priority list of Indian military assets, but confirming the presence of specific aircraft, missile systems, and logistical convoys was essential before launching any strike. Thermal imaging, signal intercepts, and even drone-mounted laser designators were used to lock in precise coordinates. These UAVs hovered over targets for hours—collecting patterns, monitoring movement, and ensuring that any strike would hit enemy military capacity, not civilian infrastructure.

In some cases, decoy drones were deployed to provoke Indian radar systems and observe response patterns. This provided valuable insight into which Indian air defense networks were active and which sectors were under-defended. In one notable instance, a drone sortie over the outskirts of Adampur Airbase detected irregular heat signatures suggesting mobile missile launchers. This intelligence led to the relocation of strike assets and the inclusion of that sector in the final strike plan.

Reconnaissance flights were also executed using manned aircraft, including the Saab Erieye airborne early warning and control systems (AEW&C), and Falcon DA-20 electronic warfare aircraft. These aircraft operated in coordination with drones to provide layered battlefield awareness. The Erieye system, mounted on Saab 2000 platforms, offered deep surveillance into Indian territory, tracking aircraft movement, refueling tankers, and identifying hidden supply lines. The combination of drones and AEW&C platforms allowed Pakistan to form a dynamic, real-time tactical map of the region.

To ensure operational secrecy, the recon data gathered by drones was transmitted using encrypted frequency-hopping communication systems. Only top-tier command units had access to live drone feeds, minimizing the risk of leaks or interference. Drone operators worked in shifts, many stationed at airbases and forward control units, operating consoles inside mobile trailers or bunkered facilities. Each operator was trained not just in flying the UAV, but in interpreting intelligence, identifying threats, and working closely with target acquisition teams.

Importantly, Pakistan's drone doctrine during Operation Bunyan-ul-Marsoos emphasized zero civilian exposure. All recon flights avoided urban or religious sites and maintained ethical protocols that aligned with both national military law and international humanitarian standards. This allowed Pakistan to maintain the moral high ground and reduce the risk of misidentification or accidental collateral damage.

The integration of drone data into the larger operational strategy was crucial. In real-time briefings at GHQ and PAF Command, drone footage was played on large tactical screens, synchronized with ground reports and satellite images. Commanders could observe patterns, identify vulnerabilities, and issue commands based on live intelligence. This responsiveness was critical in timing the strikes: Pakistan had to hit when enemy assets were exposed but before they were moved, shielded, or relocated.

Perhaps the most striking success of drone surveillance during the operation was its role in preventing escalation. By monitoring India's military posture continuously, Pakistan was able to confirm that India was not preparing for immediate follow-up strikes. This allowed the leadership to limit its retaliation to targeted military assets, avoiding a wider conflict while still delivering an unforgettable message of deterrence.

In conclusion, the use of drone surveillance and recon flights during Operation Bunyan-ul-Marsoos transformed Pakistan's response from reactive to intelligently proactive. It was not just about hitting targets — it was about knowing where, when, and why to strike, all while maintaining control, legality, and strategic clarity. In the silent sky, drones became the eyes of the nation — watching, waiting, and guiding Pakistan's silent thunder.

## Coordinated Air Strikes Begin

With surveillance complete, targets confirmed, and the operational command structure synchronized, the final phase of Operation Bunyan-ul-Marsoos was ready for execution. This was the moment Pakistan had prepared for—not to escalate, but to retaliate with power, precision, and purpose. The coordinated air strikes that followed were not only a demonstration of military capability but a symbol of strategic maturity. They marked a new chapter in Pakistan's military doctrine—one where restraint and resolve operated hand in hand.

The first wave of air strikes commenced just before dawn on May 11, 2025, approximately 48 hours after India's unprovoked missile attacks. In military terms, this was a swift response—planned meticulously and launched with surgical timing. The Pakistan Air Force (PAF) scrambled multiple JF-17 Thunder, F-16 Fighting Falcon, and Mirage-V squadrons from various airbases including PAF Base Masroor, PAF Base Shahbaz, and PAF Base Sargodha. Each pilot had rehearsed their mission dozens of times through simulations and war games. But this was no drill—this was the real thing.

The first targets were Indian military installations identified in earlier briefings: Pathankot Airbase, Adampur Airbase, and BrahMos missile storage facilities in Beas and Nagrota. These sites were chosen for their operational significance, risk reduction potential, and psychological value. Intelligence feeds from drones and satellite imagery confirmed optimal strike windows—times when high-value targets such as fuel trucks, ammunition convoys, or parked aircraft were vulnerable. The PAF didn't just strike randomly—it struck with real-time data coordination, aided by airborne early warning systems like the Saab Erieye.

The strike teams were divided into phased formations. The first group consisted of SEAD (Suppression of Enemy Air Defenses) aircraft that targeted radar installations and surface-to-air missile batteries using electronic jamming and precision-guided munitions. Clearing the path for the second wave, the SEAD aircraft blinded Indian early-warning systems for critical minutes, allowing strike formations to move in undetected.

The second group carried out the primary bombing runs, launching laser-guided and GPS-guided bombs onto hardened aircraft shelters, fuel storage tanks, and logistics hubs. The PAF used smart munitions, including the indigenous RA'AD II air-launched cruise missile, designed to minimize collateral damage while maximizing target impact. In a few cases, standoff weapons were used from outside Indian airspace to avoid provocation beyond the intended message.

The coordination didn't stop in the air. Ground command teams tracked the aircraft in real time using a secure tactical network, while intelligence officers provided live updates on any changes at the strike zones. Simultaneously, electronic warfare units jammed Indian communications, ensuring that any emergency counter-response would be delayed or misdirected. The Pakistani Navy, though not directly involved in the strikes, maintained a high-alert posture in the Arabian Sea to monitor any naval mobilization or submarine activity from India's Western Fleet.

In most strike zones, the entire operation—from ingress to target hit and egress—was completed in under 12 minutes, a testament to both the training and discipline of PAF pilots. Once the strike aircraft returned safely to Pakistani airspace, drones were deployed once again to conduct battle damage assessments (BDA). These assessments confirmed multiple direct hits, including the destruction of fuel depots at Pathankot, aircraft shelters at Adampur, and BrahMos storage bunkers in Beas. No significant civilian damage or casualties were reported, and all pilots returned without engagement from enemy aircraft.

What made these air strikes exceptional was not just their effectiveness, but their precision and proportionality. Pakistan had proven it could penetrate Indian defenses, hit critical assets, and return unharmed—without attacking civilian infrastructure or igniting a full-scale war. It was a response wrapped in discipline, bound by legality, and carried out with unwavering professionalism.

The global reaction to the strikes was immediate. While Indian media accused Pakistan of aggression, international observers took a more nuanced view. Many acknowledged that Pakistan had shown strategic restraint by limiting its retaliation to legitimate military targets. The United Nations, China, and Turkey called for immediate de-escalation, while the United States issued a statement recognizing Pakistan's right to self-defense, urging both sides to exercise caution moving forward.

Domestically, the response to the air strikes was electric. Social media lit up with praise for the Air Force. Hashtags like #SilentThunder and #BunyanUlMarsoos trended across platforms. Citizens, long accustomed to uncertainty in times of conflict, expressed pride and reassurance in their military's capability. Mosques, homes, and public spaces echoed with prayers of gratitude. Pakistan had responded—not with chaos, but with clarity.

In the end, the coordinated air strikes of Operation Bunyan-ul-Marsoos achieved far more than their physical impact. They restored deterrence, rebuilt confidence, and redefined how modern Pakistan conducts warfare. This was not just retaliation—it was a statement: Pakistan is ready, capable, and resolute—guided by discipline, not desperation.

# Chapter 5
# Breaking the Myth of Invincibility

For decades, India projected an aura of military superiority in the South Asian region—backed by global partnerships, advanced weapon systems, and a narrative of technological dominance. This perception, amplified by media and often reinforced by Western defense circles, portrayed India as a near-invincible regional power, especially in air defense and missile capability. But Operation Bunyan-ul-Marsoos would shatter that illusion with surgical precision.

This chapter focuses on how Pakistan's coordinated retaliatory strikes exposed the vulnerabilities of India's most critical military assets. The successful engagement of Pathankot and Adampur airbases—both strategic hubs for northern command operations—demonstrated not only Pakistan's reach but its operational excellence. These were not soft or symbolic targets. They were fortified bases with layered defenses, yet Pakistani jets penetrated them with stealth and accuracy.

Perhaps even more revealing was the destruction of BrahMos missile storage sites in Beas and Nagrota. The BrahMos, a symbol of

India's strike-first doctrine and deterrence capability, was considered untouchable—until it wasn't. The elimination of these assets sent a powerful message: technological superiority means little if it cannot be protected.

Finally, Pakistan's ability to neutralize components of the S-400 air defense system, long considered one of the most advanced in the world, delivered a psychological and strategic shock. Purchased from Russia and touted as a game-changer, the S-400 failed to intercept or deter Pakistan's precision strikes.

This chapter breaks down how Operation Bunyan-ul-Marsoos did more than retaliate—it unraveled a myth. It reminded the region and the world that true strength lies not just in possession, but in preparation, unity, and execution.

## Strike on Pathankot and Adampur

The strikes on Pathankot and Adampur airbases during Operation Bunyan-ul-Marsoos marked a critical turning point in South Asia's strategic balance. These were not ordinary targets. Located in India's Punjab state, both bases form the backbone of India's northern air defense posture. They house advanced fighter squadrons, surveillance systems, and serve as rapid deployment hubs for operations across the western border. For years, they were seen as fortified, well-defended, and largely immune to external threats. But on the early morning of May 11, 2025, that illusion was shattered.

The decision to strike these specific locations stemmed from multiple strategic considerations. First, both bases had played a **direct logistical role** in India's earlier missile attacks on Pakistani airbases. Surveillance and signals intelligence confirmed that key support aircraft and mobile missile units were recently active at both sites. Second, their proximity to Pakistan made them tactically accessible while still being politically and militarily significant. Lastly, by targeting assets at these two high-value locations, Pakistan aimed to undermine the perception of India's invulnerability.

The operation began just before dawn. A coordinated squadron of JF-17 Thunder and Mirage-V aircraft, supported by electronic warfare teams and aerial early warning systems, launched from multiple PAF bases. The plan was to conduct simultaneous multi-angle strikes that would overwhelm Indian air defenses and achieve maximum damage within the shortest window possible. The attack plan followed a three-phase model: suppression of air defenses, primary target strikes, and rapid exfiltration.

At Pathankot Airbase, the primary objective was to neutralize fuel storage facilities, aircraft shelters, and satellite communication nodes. Pakistani aircraft used precision-guided munitions (PGMs) to avoid unnecessary collateral damage. Surveillance drones and laser designators ensured target accuracy in real time. A secondary explosion was observed minutes after the strike, indicating that munitions or fuel stocks had been successfully ignited. Satellite imagery released later confirmed at least three hardened aircraft shelters were damaged and two fuel tankers destroyed.

Meanwhile, at Adampur Airbase, the focus was on grounded aircraft and missile storage bunkers. Real-time intelligence suggested a squadron of Su-30 MKI aircraft had been temporarily repositioned there after the initial Indian attack on Pakistan. Pakistani strike jets approached from the southwest under radar cover, launched stand-off weapons, and pulled away before Indian air defenses could fully respond. The success of this mission hinged on jamming Indian radar systems and timing the attack with drone-based surveillance that had confirmed low aerial activity at the time.

One of the most remarkable aspects of these strikes was the **coordination and speed** with which they were executed. The total operation time—ingress, strike, and return—lasted **under 14 minutes**. Not a single PAF jet was downed, and no direct air-to-air engagement occurred. India's early-warning systems were **blinded or bypassed**, and by the time ground defenses responded, Pakistani aircraft had already returned to home base.

The psychological impact of the strikes on Pathankot and Adampur was as significant as the physical damage. For years, India had projected these bases as central pillars of its air superiority. They were regularly showcased in military drills, documentaries, and media briefings. The belief that these installations could withstand any aerial intrusion was widely held by both Indian defense planners and the general public. Operation Bunyan-ul-Marsoos punctured that narrative.

Indian media initially downplayed the extent of the damage. However, satellite imagery released by independent defense analysts soon revealed scorched runways, smoke plumes, and disrupted tarmac activity at both airfields. Reports emerged that certain flight operations were redirected to alternate bases in the days following the attack, a further indication of operational disruption.

From Pakistan's perspective, the strikes on Pathankot and Adampur were more than tactical victories. They served to:

1. Demonstrate precision capability – proving that Pakistan could strike high-value military targets with minimal collateral damage.
2. Expose Indian vulnerabilities – highlighting that even heavily defended bases were not immune to well-planned attacks.
3. Re-establish deterrence – by signaling that Pakistan would respond decisively and effectively to aggression.

International reactions were mixed. While some Western powers urged restraint, military observers quietly acknowledged the efficiency and discipline of the strikes. Even neutral analysts admitted that Pakistan had executed a technically complex operation with strategic finesse, challenging the long-standing perception of asymmetry in air capability.

Ultimately, the strikes on Pathankot and Adampur were not merely acts of retaliation—they were a strategic narrative reset. They showed that Pakistan's air force, guided by intelligence, empowered by technology, and united under a clear command, could break through layers of defense, strike where it mattered, and return without provocation or panic.

The myth of India's untouchable northern air defense had been dismantled—in under fifteen minutes.

## BrahMos Storage Sites: A Tactical Blow

Among the most significant achievements of Operation Bunyan-ul-Marsoos was the successful targeting and neutralization of BrahMos missile storage facilities in Beas and Nagrota. These sites held strategic value far beyond their physical footprint. The

BrahMos missile, a joint development between India and Russia, is widely regarded as one of the fastest and most advanced supersonic cruise missiles in the world. It forms the backbone of India's precision strike capability and is integral to its "Cold Start" doctrine. By striking these storage sites, Pakistan delivered a tactical and psychological blow to India's sense of strategic invincibility.

Prior to the strike, Pakistan's intelligence community, particularly the Inter-Services Intelligence (ISI) and Air Intelligence units, had been closely monitoring the transport and positioning of BrahMos launchers and stockpiles. Signals intelligence (SIGINT) and high-resolution satellite imagery showed increased activity in storage depots near Beas (Punjab) and Nagrota (Jammu & Kashmir). Truck convoys, satellite uplinks, and the presence of Russian-supplied maintenance crews indicated that these locations were housing live or soon-to-be-deployed missiles.

What made these sites prime targets was not just the presence of advanced weaponry, but their integration into India's forward-strike infrastructure. The BrahMos system, with its ability to deliver a high-speed, low-altitude strike with exceptional accuracy, poses a credible threat to Pakistan's military installations. By taking out these assets early, Pakistan achieved two things: it eliminated a pressing threat and sent a strong message that even India's most guarded technologies were not beyond reach.

The operation to strike the BrahMos depots began in the early hours of May 11, as part of the second wave of coordinated air sorties under Operation Bunyan-ul-Marsoos. JF-17 Thunder jets, armed with stand-off weapons and supported by electronic warfare aircraft, were assigned to carry out the mission. These aircraft launched from PAF Base Rafiqui and were guided in real time by drone surveillance and AWACS platforms that monitored enemy radar systems.

At the Beas site, located in the heart of Punjab, the primary target was a heavily guarded storage bunker believed to hold multiple BrahMos missile canisters. The approach vector was carefully chosen to avoid detection by India's layered radar defenses. The strike aircraft released laser-guided munitions and cruise missiles from a distance, allowing them to remain outside enemy airspace. The precision strike ignited a series of secondary explosions, confirming the destruction of ammunition or fuel within the compound. Thermal imaging from surveillance drones showed a rapid rise in temperature followed by a large-scale fire—an unmistakable sign of a successful hit.

Meanwhile, the Nagrota depot, located near the LoC and critical to India's Northern Command operations, posed a unique challenge. It was nestled in hilly terrain and guarded with reinforced concrete bunkers. However, persistent drone surveillance over the previous 72 hours had revealed loading operations, suggesting imminent missile deployment. Timing was critical. The Pakistani strike aircraft employed smart bombs with deep-penetration warheads, designed to break through hardened structures. The result was devastating: multiple underground storage units were destroyed, and key logistical buildings collapsed under the force of the blasts.

Both strikes were executed with minimal collateral damage, as verified by post-strike surveillance. Civilian infrastructure and surrounding areas were untouched. This level of accuracy bolstered Pakistan's standing on the international stage and demonstrated its commitment to military professionalism and rules of engagement.

The destruction of the BrahMos sites had immediate tactical implications. India was forced to suspend plans for additional missile deployment along the western border. Maintenance teams were relocated, and military assets were dispersed to avoid further strikes. The psychological impact was equally potent: a weapon system once considered untouchable had been struck—effectively and publicly.

The blow also sent a signal to India's strategic partners. The BrahMos program is not only an indigenous capability but also a symbol of India's growing defense ties with Russia and its ambitions for regional dominance. Pakistan's ability to identify, target, and destroy these facilities undermined that narrative. It demonstrated that advanced weaponry without proper concealment or defense is a liability, not a strength.

International military analysts, including those from neutral countries, acknowledged the significance of the strikes. Western defense think tanks noted that Pakistan had achieved a rare feat: neutralizing a top-tier missile system without triggering uncontrolled escalation. By limiting the operation to military assets and executing it with precision, Pakistan preserved its diplomatic leverage while reshaping regional threat perceptions.

In summary, the targeting of BrahMos storage sites in Beas and Nagrota was more than just a strike—it was a calculated dismantling of India's strategic posture. It erased the myth of untouchable superiority and rebalanced the psychological playing field. Operation Bunyan-ul-Marsoos had not only responded—it had redefined the rules of engagement.

## Neutralizing S-400 Air Defense Zones

One of the most pivotal achievements of Operation Bunyan-ul-Marsoos was the successful neutralization of components of India's S-400 air defense system—a feat that not only defied regional expectations but also sent ripples across the global defense community. The Russian-made S-400 Triumf, known for its advanced tracking and interception capabilities, had been touted as India's "air defense shield," capable of neutralizing airborne threats far before they breached Indian airspace. Its deployment in strategic zones was meant to deter any Pakistani response. But what unfolded during Pakistan's retaliatory campaign changed that narrative.

India had acquired the S-400 system in recent years as part of a multi-billion-dollar defense deal with Russia. The systems were deployed in three strategic sectors: the western command near Punjab, the northern command near Jammu, and parts of central India for capital defense. These systems were widely publicized as game-changing assets that would give India an edge in any aerial engagement. However, the assumption that the S-400 could blanket the entire region with invulnerability was quickly tested—and found wanting.

In preparation for Operation Bunyan-ul-Marsoos, Pakistan's military planners and electronic warfare experts had been studying the S-400 deployment patterns meticulously. Leveraging signals intelligence (SIGINT), satellite surveillance, and inputs from foreign defense analysts, the Pakistan Air Force (PAF) mapped out the system's radar arcs, blind spots, and reaction times. It was understood that while the S-400 was technologically superior, it had critical limitations—its radar coverage was not seamless, its mobility was limited once deployed, and it could be overwhelmed by decoys and electronic interference.

The strategy to counter and neutralize the S-400 was threefold:

1. **Deception and Saturation:** PAF used drone swarms and decoy aircraft to trigger S-400 radar systems in one sector while real strike aircraft maneuvered in from an alternate vector. This classic misdirection caused Indian air defense operators to allocate tracking resources to non-threats, leaving real ingress paths vulnerable.

2. **Electronic Warfare (EW):** Pakistan deployed Falcon DA-20 aircraft and other electronic warfare platforms to jam and disrupt the S-400's communication with its radar and missile units. These platforms created electronic "ghosts," spoofing the system's targeting algorithms and confusing it in moments when fast decisions were critical.

3. **Stand-Off Precision Strikes:** Once weaknesses were detected, the PAF launched air-to-surface missiles and smart bombs from stand-off distances—outside the engagement envelope of the S-400's shorter-range interceptors. These weapons were guided by real-time drone feeds and AWACS systems, ensuring they hit exact coordinates of S-400 radar vehicles, power supply units, and command modules.

The strike near Pathankot proved especially successful. Intelligence reports had confirmed the presence of an S-400 battery deployed to protect the airbase and nearby installations. During the operation, Pakistani drones simulated a slow air incursion, prompting the system to "wake up" and begin tracking. Simultaneously, jamming aircraft in the area began to blind and distort the radar signals. Within that moment of confusion, JF-17

Thunder jets launched stand-off missiles that destroyed the S-400's central radar and power systems. The system was effectively rendered inoperative for the rest of the operation.

Another significant strike occurred near Nagrota, where a mobile S-400 unit had recently been installed. The terrain had provided the system with concealment, but prolonged drone surveillance had revealed its precise location. A carefully timed precision strike using smart munitions targeted the system's launch vehicles and logistic support trucks. Satellite imagery and intercepted Indian military chatter later confirmed the destruction of multiple components.

The broader impact of neutralizing the S-400 zones was twofold:

1. **Operational Freedom:** With these key air defense umbrellas down, Pakistan's strike aircraft gained operational freedom to hit other military targets with less risk, expanding the scope of Bunyan-ul-Marsoos without requiring a wider escalation.

2. **Psychological Advantage:** The myth of the S-400's impenetrability was shattered. For India, this was more than a tactical loss—it was a strategic embarrassment. For Pakistan, it was a declaration of its technological advancement, strategic foresight, and professional execution.

Internationally, defense experts took note. Commentaries from Western think tanks acknowledged that Pakistan had achieved what many considered improbable: disabling components of one of the world's most advanced air defense systems using indigenous platforms, electronic warfare, and smart tactics. This achievement elevated Pakistan's standing in global military discourse and demonstrated that no system is invulnerable if challenged with intellect and innovation.

In the end, neutralizing the S-400 zones during Operation Bunyan-ul-Marsoos was not just a tactical win—it was a strategic dismantling of deterrence optics. Pakistan had exposed the limits of India's much-celebrated shield and proved that modern warfare is not decided by hardware alone—but by the minds that maneuver it.

# Chapter 6
# The Invisible War: Cyber & EW

While missiles soared across borders and fighter jets roared through the skies, a different kind of war was being fought in silence — one without explosions, but no less devastating. It was the war of algorithms, frequencies, firewalls, and disruption. As Pakistan launched Operation Bunyan-ul-Marsoos in the physical domain, it also unleashed a simultaneous campaign in the digital and electromagnetic spectrum, designed to disarm, destabilize, and confuse Indian military and civilian infrastructure.

This chapter explores Pakistan's multi-pronged cyber and electronic warfare (EW) operations that ran parallel to its air strikes. These efforts were meticulously planned to blind India's radar, scramble its communications, and cripple its digital backbone during critical phases of the operation — all without ever crossing a physical border.

From cyber disruptions targeting Indian power grids and military communication networks, to jamming electronic signals and suppressing radar systems, this was a silent offensive aimed at achieving maximum confusion with minimal exposure. The sophistication and coordination displayed in this arena underscored Pakistan's evolution in hybrid warfare, where the lines between the digital and kinetic battlefield have blurred.

Equally vital was the role played by Inter-Services Intelligence (ISI) and allied cyber units in shaping the information narrative. Through cyber-infiltration, psychological operations, and selective leaks, Pakistan controlled the tempo of perception — ensuring the world saw Bunyan-ul-Marsoos not as reckless aggression, but as a disciplined and lawful retaliation.

In this chapter, we dive into the invisible battlefield where dominance isn't measured in destroyed buildings, but in silenced radars, frozen systems, and minds thrown into disarray — a battlefield where victory is silent, but absolute.

## Cyber Disruption of Indian Grids and Comms

While the world's attention was riveted on the dogfights in the skies and the explosions on military bases, a quieter but equally potent war was unfolding — one fought in the shadows of code, servers, and data streams. During Operation Bunyan-ul-Marsoos, Pakistan launched a highly coordinated cyber offensive targeting critical Indian infrastructure, command systems, and digital communications. This invisible dimension of the conflict aimed not to destroy, but to disorient, delay, and destabilize — and it proved remarkably effective.

Pakistan's cyber strategy was designed around targeted disruption, not total annihilation. The objective was to create just enough interference in India's military and civil networks to impede operational tempo, trigger internal confusion, and delay counter-response coordination — all without provoking uncontrolled escalation. The cyber offensive began hours before the first Pakistani fighter jet entered Indian airspace, timed meticulously to soften digital defenses before physical strikes commenced.

The **primary targets** of the cyber disruption campaign included:

1. **Military Communication Networks** – Secure Indian Army and Air Force communication nodes, especially those relaying real-time data to air defense units, were targeted with denial-of-service (DoS) and data spoofing attacks. This led to delays in transmitting vital targeting information and resulted in temporary blind spots during Pakistan's aerial strike windows.

2. **Air Traffic and Radar Coordination Systems** – Pakistan's cyber units, in collaboration with specialized military electronic warfare teams, disrupted select civilian and military radar grids. Several regional flight tracking systems experienced blackouts, with both military and commercial aircraft rerouted or grounded due to temporary chaos in airspace management.

3. **Energy Grids and Substations** – While full-scale blackouts were avoided, power fluctuations and control panel malfunctions were reported in at least three northern Indian substations, two of which were believed to supply power to nearby military installations. These micro-disruptions did not cripple energy supply, but they added a layer of complexity to the already stressed Indian infrastructure.

4. **Emergency Response Networks** – Some Indian emergency communication platforms, particularly those operated by state governments near the border, were briefly overloaded

or rendered unresponsive. This caused confusion at the local level, with delayed instructions being relayed to disaster and medical response units.

The execution of these attacks pointed to a high level of planning and access, with cyber operatives exploiting known vulnerabilities in India's legacy IT systems and critical infrastructure. In several cases, sleeper malware previously planted in routine phishing attacks was activated remotely to overload or bypass firewalls. These operations were not random; they were based on pre-mapped vulnerabilities, identified and cataloged in months leading up to the conflict.

Reports from cybersecurity firms and Indian IT watchdogs post-strike confirmed that the intrusions were "highly coordinated," involving advanced persistent threats (APTs) and zero-day exploits. These were not amateur hacks but military-grade intrusions, designed to remain undetected, execute a task, and vanish without leaving behind actionable forensics.

Interestingly, while the cyber disruptions created panic and delay, they stopped short of causing mass civilian harm — a calculated decision by Pakistan's command to remain within the bounds of international cyber law and avoid civilian outrage. This discipline maintained Pakistan's moral and strategic upper hand in the information war.

Pakistan's Cyber Warfare Division, working under the Strategic Plans Division (SPD), led the technical operations. However, it was the collaboration with intelligence agencies like ISI, which provided on-ground and signal-based intelligence, that made the operations precise. The synergy between cyber, signal intelligence, and kinetic action allowed Pakistan to degrade Indian coordination at multiple levels — right as fighter jets entered their final strike formation.

The psychological effect of the cyber disruptions was as powerful as the technical outcome. Indian military command and political leaders were left guessing: Were the communication breakdowns due to technical failure, internal errors, or external attack? This confusion bought Pakistan crucial minutes of operational freedom, allowed air strike teams to move with minimal resistance, and fed uncertainty into India's planning loop.

International cyber analysts were quick to take notice. Several global threat-monitoring platforms recorded unusual network behavior across northern India. While Indian media attempted to downplay the extent of damage, cyber threat intelligence agencies in the West flagged Operation Bunyan-ul-Marsoos as an example of next-generation hybrid warfare — where cyber attacks act as force multipliers for conventional military action.

The cyber disruption of Indian grids and communication systems during Operation Bunyan-ul-Marsoos was not just a supporting tactic — it was a strategic pillar of the operation. It exemplified Pakistan's growing capability in asymmetric digital warfare, its understanding of modern battlefields, and its ability to use invisible tools to win very real victories. In this silent war, no buildings were bombed, but walls of certainty were dismantled. In a matter of minutes, Pakistan proved that dominance is not just about firepower — it's about foresight, finesse, and control.

## Electronic Warfare: Jammed and Blinded

While Pakistan's air force thundered through the skies during Operation Bunyan-ul-Marsoos, another equally vital and invisible force was at work below the radar—electronic warfare (EW). The precision and success of Pakistan's retaliatory strikes were not achieved through firepower alone, but through a meticulously orchestrated electromagnetic campaign that disoriented Indian defenses, scrambled their response networks, and rendered key systems temporarily blind.

Electronic Warfare refers to the strategic use of electromagnetic energy to detect, deceive, disrupt, or destroy the enemy's radar and communication capabilities. In Bunyan-ul-Marsoos, Pakistan's EW units executed one of the most complex and synchronized jamming operations in the country's history, demonstrating that the first shots of modern warfare are often fired silently—through interference, not explosions.

The EW mission had three core objectives:

1. Disable Indian radar systems and early warning networks.
2. Jam and intercept command-and-control communications.
3. Create operational corridors for Pakistani aircraft to enter and exit Indian airspace undetected.

At the heart of Pakistan's EW operations were platforms like the DA-20 Falcon aircraft, equipped with signal jamming pods, electronic support measures (ESM), and signal intelligence (SIGINT) tools. These aircraft flew in tandem with strike formations, acting as a shield of silence by emitting high-power signals to disrupt Indian radar systems and scramble enemy transmissions. At the same time, ground-based mobile jamming units, deployed near the Line of Control and strategic points in Punjab, were activated to suppress Indian radio frequencies and military channels.

In the Pathankot-Adampur sector, EW teams successfully executed coordinated jamming missions that neutralized Indian S-band and L-band radar coverage for several minutes. This brief blackout was crucial—it provided the Pakistani jets with a narrow but exploitable window to ingress, release their payloads, and egress without being tracked or intercepted. Radar operators on the Indian side, facing static noise and misaligned tracking signals, were left momentarily disoriented, unsure whether they were looking at a real threat or ghost echoes.

Furthermore, frequency-hopping communication between Indian command centers and field units—designed to be resilient—was also temporarily disrupted. Pakistani EW units, using pre-mapped signal libraries and digital intercepts, were able to jam or imitate Indian military communications, causing confusion in transmission sequences. In some instances, false signals were inserted into enemy channels, delaying response coordination and spreading doubt about the integrity of orders.

Another critical target of the EW campaign was air defense batteries. India's surface-to-air missile (SAM) systems—particularly in areas near BrahMos sites and northern airbases—depend on radar guidance and central command coordination. By jamming uplink signals and confusing radar locks, Pakistani EW teams were able to dilute the effectiveness of Indian missile defenses, allowing strike aircraft to operate within a safer margin.

The electronic assault was not limited to military installations alone. Dual-use infrastructure—such as air traffic control systems and civilian aviation communication nodes—was also impacted in a controlled and time-bound manner. While no civilian aircraft were endangered, brief and selective interference disrupted routine flight tracking and regional airspace management, causing further confusion in an already high-stakes environment.

Behind this sophisticated operation was a network of signal intelligence analysts, software engineers, and battlefield technologists working closely with the Strategic Plans Division and the Air Force's EW Command. These teams had spent years preparing for scenarios exactly like this—conducting simulations, gathering spectral intelligence, and building a database of Indian signal profiles. The success of the mission was a testament not just to Pakistan's hardware capabilities, but its data-driven electronic warfare doctrine.

The psychological effect of being electronically blinded cannot be overstated. Indian commanders found themselves struggling to communicate, to detect, to respond. The uncertainty that EW attacks generate can often paralyze decision-making. In this case, the fog of war was created not by smoke, but by silence—and that silence was engineered by Pakistan.

International observers were quick to note the sophistication of the EW component in Bunyan-ul-Marsoos. Defense analysts from NATO and Asia-Pacific think tanks highlighted how Pakistan had used electronic warfare not just as a support element but as a primary enabler of its kinetic strikes. This integration of soft disruption with hard retaliation represented a paradigm shift in South Asian military engagements.

The "jamming and blinding" of India's critical radar and communication networks during Operation Bunyan-ul-Marsoos underscored a new era of warfare. It proved that modern conflicts are no longer won solely by bombs and bullets, but by control over the unseen battlespace—the electromagnetic spectrum. Pakistan's ability to dominate that spectrum turned the tide of battle before the first missile ever left the wing.

## ISI's Role in Info Ops

In modern warfare, shaping perceptions is just as critical as winning battles. The Inter-Services Intelligence (ISI), Pakistan's premier intelligence agency, played a central role during Operation Bunyan-ul-Marsoos not only in providing intelligence and surveillance but also in leading the information operations (Info Ops) that influenced global narratives, controlled internal morale, and undermined Indian confidence. While fighter jets, drones, and electronic warfare made headlines, it was the ISI's invisible hand that ensured Pakistan controlled the story of the war.

The ISI's Info Ops campaign was multi-layered, covering three main objectives:

1. Manage the domestic narrative to preserve unity and morale.
2. Shape the international perception to legitimize Pakistan's response.
3. Disrupt and confuse Indian public discourse and media cohesion.

### Domestic Information Dominance

Internally, Pakistan faced the critical task of keeping public sentiment steady, avoiding panic, and maintaining trust in the military's response. From the outset, the ISI, in coordination with the military's Inter-Services Public Relations (ISPR), managed a carefully calibrated media and messaging strategy. National television networks, radio, and social media were mobilized to deliver real-time updates that emphasized discipline, preparedness, and moral high ground.

News anchors echoed the government's measured tone. Military experts were selectively briefed to appear on national broadcasts to explain Pakistan's strategic restraint, while simultaneously assuring that any aggression would be met with strength. The ISI also worked with civil authorities to prevent the spread of false alarms or unverified news through WhatsApp groups and Facebook pages by deploying cyber monitoring units and pushing rapid counter-narratives.

Cultural messaging was also utilized. Religious scholars and public figures were engaged to reinforce themes of unity, faith, and national resilience. In mosques and community centers, references to Bunyan-ul-Marsoos — a wall of steel — were invoked to create a psychological bulwark against fear. This internal information stability allowed the military to operate without civilian unrest or loss of public confidence.

**International Messaging and Diplomatic Narrative**

On the global front, the ISI worked in tandem with the Foreign Office to frame Operation Bunyan-ul-Marsoos as a lawful, proportionate act of self-defense under Article 51 of the United Nations Charter. Intelligence gathered from diplomatic channels, international media monitors, and allied embassies was fed back to the Foreign Office, allowing Pakistan to tailor its messaging to various global audiences — from Washington and Beijing to Riyadh and Ankara.

Through strategic leaks to international journalists and think tanks, the ISI ensured that foreign analysts had access to non-classified evidence of Indian provocation, including satellite imagery of Indian missile deployments and command movements prior to the initial attack. Carefully selected international media outlets received pre-cleared briefings showing that Pakistan's response was targeted, precise, and deliberately limited to avoid escalation.

In Western capitals, this narrative resonated. While some governments urged restraint, few condemned Pakistan outright — a notable shift from previous conflicts. This was a direct result of the quiet but assertive information diplomacy orchestrated by the ISI and its diplomatic counterparts.

**Psychological Operations and Indian Disruption**

Perhaps the most subtle yet impactful component of ISI's role was its psychological operations (psy-ops) targeting Indian military morale and public perception. Using a mix of cyber infiltration, AI-generated messaging, and digital influence campaigns, the ISI sowed confusion in Indian media and social platforms during and after the strikes.

Bot networks amplified hashtags that questioned the Indian government's preparedness, exaggerated internal dissent, and spread doubt about the performance of Indian air defenses, particularly the S-400 system. Leaked communications, possibly real or fabricated, were disseminated to suggest disunity among Indian command circles and to create an illusion of internal chaos.

The ISI's cyber division also launched spoof attacks on Indian military social media accounts, injecting false alerts and contradicting official narratives. Some of these were quickly debunked, but the initial moment of confusion they caused was enough to raise public skepticism within India. Even respected Indian media outlets found themselves struggling to verify reports, leading to conflicting versions of events — a classic success in information warfare.

The ISI also operated through non-official cover agents and proxies in regional think tanks and media circles across South Asia, subtly influencing opinion pieces, panel discussions, and editorials. In this way, even neutral commentators began to highlight Pakistan's professionalism and question India's strategic decisions.

The ISI's role in Info Ops during Operation Bunyan-ul-Marsoos was not merely supportive — it was central to the success of the mission. By controlling the flow of information, influencing perception, and neutralizing hostile narratives, the ISI ensured that Pakistan won not just the war in the air, but the battle for minds. In an era where wars are fought as much through screens as through weapons, the ISI proved that mastery over information is now as decisive as dominance on the battlefield.

# Chapter 7
# Civilian Shield, Military Spear

While fighter jets executed precision strikes and digital warfare scrambled enemy systems, the heart of Pakistan—its people—remained both vulnerable and vital. As Operation Bunyan-ul-Marsoos escalated, it became clear that victory was not only about military supremacy in the skies, but also about maintaining internal stability, protecting civilians, and preserving public confidence. In the backdrop of regional tension and potential full-scale war, Pakistan's leadership undertook a crucial parallel mission: to safeguard its urban centers and shield its population from psychological and physical fallout.

This chapter explores how the state mobilized a comprehensive civil-military strategy that elevated homeland security to the same level of importance as frontline operations. Pakistan's major cities—Islamabad, Lahore, Karachi, Peshawar, and Rawalpindi—were identified as potential high-value targets, not only because of their strategic significance, but also due to their symbolic weight. The government and armed forces, working in lockstep, established contingency shelters, emergency drills, early warning systems, and air defense coordination around civilian infrastructure.

At the same time, internal cohesion became a national objective. From local governments to religious leaders and the media, the ISPR and civilian authorities worked hand-in-hand to foster national unity. Preventing panic, dispelling rumors, and reinforcing messages of resilience were critical tasks, carried out with remarkable speed and coordination.

This chapter also examines the media's role—not just as a communication tool, but as a force multiplier for morale. With the nation under pressure, Pakistan's information apparatus performed the delicate balancing act of transparency without fear-mongering, ensuring that the public stayed informed, alert, and unbroken.

Here, the people were not passive bystanders. They became the shield behind the spear, the spirit that powered the precision—and the soul of the nation's defense.

## Protecting Urban Centers During Escalation

In the midst of Operation Bunyan-ul-Marsoos, as Pakistani fighter jets delivered a calibrated military response to Indian aggression, a parallel and no less critical mission unfolded across the nation's cities: the protection of civilian life and infrastructure. From Islamabad's diplomatic quarter to Karachi's industrial sprawl, urban centers became strategic fronts where the stakes were high and the margin for error razor-thin. The protection of these centers was not merely a humanitarian concern—it was essential to maintaining national morale, preventing chaos, and denying the enemy any psychological victory.

From the moment it became clear that a regional conflict was brewing, Pakistan's National Security Council (NSC), in coordination with the Pakistan Armed Forces and National Disaster

Management Authority (NDMA), activated pre-established urban defense protocols. These were not created in haste; they were the result of years of strategic planning, shaped by previous crises and evolving regional threats. Operation Bunyan-ul-Marsoos marked the first time these protocols were tested in real combat conditions—and they held.

### Early Warning and Rapid Mobilization

The cornerstone of urban defense during escalation was the national early warning system, which linked military radar and air defense networks with civilian emergency response units. This system ensured that any aerial threat approaching Pakistani airspace could be assessed, tracked, and communicated to city administrations within seconds. Sirens, mass text alerts, and live television/radio interruptions were used to notify the public when to take cover, while pre-designated public shelters—including basements of schools, mosques, and government buildings—were activated as safe zones.

Metro areas like Lahore and Peshawar, considered potential targets due to their proximity to the eastern border, were temporarily put under civil-military lockdowns during high-risk windows. Non-essential movement was restricted, hospitals went on high alert, and civil defense volunteers were activated to guide citizens to safety in densely populated areas.

### Strategic Civil Infrastructure Hardening

One of the most underreported yet significant aspects of the urban defense plan was the hardening of key infrastructure—including power plants, communication nodes, water reservoirs, and transportation hubs. This involved deploying portable air defense units around critical installations and reinforcing physical barriers to protect against both conventional and drone attacks. Karachi's port, the backbone of national commerce, was temporarily rerouted for military logistics, while Islamabad's Red Zone received layered defense from both ground-based and airborne security teams.

Additionally, public utilities were decentralized where possible, to ensure that if one node failed, backup generators, water lines, and communication channels could seamlessly carry the load. This redundancy prevented a city-wide blackout or communications paralysis—a vital edge in maintaining order during tense moments.

**Coordination Between Civil and Military Leadership**

What set this effort apart was the unprecedented coordination between military commanders and local administrators. Military field officers were embedded within provincial disaster management cells to ensure real-time information exchange. Local police forces received additional training in managing crowds during air raid alerts, while hospital administrators worked with military medics to prepare for mass casualty scenarios—fortunately never realized due to the effectiveness of deterrence and defense.

This civil-military cooperation extended to the neighborhood level. Union councils and municipal committees were briefed and equipped to conduct community drills, distribute emergency supplies, and conduct door-to-door safety checks in low-income areas where access to mass communication was limited. These grassroots efforts gave every citizen a stake in national defense, transforming fear into collective responsibility.

### Maintaining Public Order and Morale

Protecting urban centers wasn't just about intercepting missiles or building bunkers—it was also about managing fear. The Inter-Services Public Relations (ISPR) division, in collaboration with mainstream media and social platforms, launched a coordinated campaign that delivered accurate updates, debunked rumors, and shared uplifting stories of resilience and patriotism. Public service announcements featured respected voices—religious leaders, artists, athletes—who urged calm, unity, and preparedness.

Volunteer youth groups and NGOs distributed food and emergency kits in vulnerable neighborhoods, while schools and universities, though closed temporarily, became centers of relief coordination. The tone was not of panic, but of stoic preparedness.

The message was clear: Pakistan would not allow its civilians to become soft targets or symbols of vulnerability. The defense of its cities was as important as the retaliation in the skies. And in doing so, the nation sent a strong message to its adversary—you may strike with machines, but our resolve is human and unbreakable.

## Internal Security Measures and Unity

As Operation Bunyan-ul-Marsoos unfolded with precision strikes and a strong retaliatory posture, Pakistan's internal security landscape was placed on high alert. The military's response to external aggression needed to be supported by flawless internal cohesion—not just in terms of law enforcement, but in preserving social order, economic stability, and public unity during a period of extreme national tension. What followed was one of the most well-coordinated internal security operations in Pakistan's recent history.

The National Counter Terrorism Authority (NACTA) and Interior Ministry, in close coordination with the Inter-Services Intelligence (ISI) and the Military Intelligence (MI), executed a country-wide directive that placed urban centers, strategic installations, transport infrastructure, and sensitive religious or political sites under protective monitoring. The objectives were clear:

1. Prevent internal sabotage, panic, or subversive activity.
2. Maintain unity among diverse communities.
3. Support the military's external operations by ensuring a secure and stable internal front.

**City-Wide Surveillance and Rapid Response Units**

In the early hours following the initiation of Pakistan's aerial strikes, Rapid Response Forces (RRF) were deployed across major cities. These highly mobile units, comprising both military and police personnel, were tasked with neutralizing any signs of coordinated chaos—whether it came from external sympathizers, radical elements, or criminal groups seeking to exploit the situation. Security was intensified around embassies, media houses, power grids, and railway stations.

The Safe City Projects in Islamabad, Lahore, and Karachi—previously seen as surveillance tools—became force multipliers. Real-time monitoring via thousands of CCTV cameras enabled swift tracking of suspicious activity, vehicle movements, and crowd behavior. Geo-fencing and telecom triangulation were also employed to track persons of interest previously flagged by intelligence agencies.

## Border Security and Anti-Infiltration Measures

Alongside urban deployments, Pakistan's paramilitary forces, including the Rangers and Frontier Corps, were mobilized along both the eastern and western borders to ensure that no cross-border infiltration or sabotage attempts could succeed. While the primary threat came from the Indian front, there was also concern that hostile third-party actors might use the opportunity to destabilize Pakistan internally.

The ISI, in particular, maintained a high-alert status in Balochistan and Khyber Pakhtunkhwa, where anti-state elements have historically exploited moments of national crisis. Dozens of intelligence-based operations (IBOs) were quietly carried out to preempt any attacks on infrastructure, communication lines, or military convoys. These efforts helped prevent a two-front scenario—one external and one internal—from ever materializing.

## Religious Harmony and Inter-Sect Coordination

Periods of national security stress are often exploited by those seeking to divide a nation along sectarian or ethnic lines. But in the case of Bunyan-ul-Marsoos, Pakistan's security and religious institutions demonstrated rare unity and proactive engagement. The Council of Islamic Ideology (CII) and Wafaq-ul-Madaris issued unified statements urging religious harmony, denouncing any acts of internal violence, and calling on scholars of all sects to promote patriotism over division.

Mosques, Imambargahs, churches, and temples were placed under protective surveillance, but also turned into community centers of resilience. Clerics across the country offered prayers for the armed forces, held peace vigils, and reminded the faithful that Pakistan's strength lay in its diversity and solidarity.

## Public Unity and Volunteer Networks

Beyond military and police action, a powerful force was mobilized: the will of the people. Volunteer groups, youth organizations, university alumni circles, and charity foundations created a nationwide web of civil assistance. These groups distributed emergency supplies, blood donations, and helped elderly citizens during curfews or siren drills.

In cities like Peshawar and Quetta—often seen as vulnerable—civilians stepped forward to assist local police in manning checkpoints, coordinating with rescue services, and maintaining queues at petrol stations and grocery stores. Rather than descending into fear, Pakistanis embraced discipline, awareness, and shared responsibility.

Social media, often a double-edged sword, was used constructively as well. ISPR's consistent updates, short videos of soldier morale, and community response footage became viral symbols of unity. Citizens were encouraged to verify news before sharing, report rumors, and use national emergency apps like PakAlert to stay informed.

## Economic and Institutional Stability

Recognizing the potential for economic disruption, the State Bank of Pakistan, in coordination with the Ministry of Finance, announced measures to ensure liquidity, digital transaction continuity, and price monitoring. Military logistics supported fuel convoys, and the army's supply chain was used to deliver goods to regions cut off due to precautionary roadblocks.

Universities, courts, and government offices adjusted their operations but remained functional under limited schedules—projecting a national image of controlled continuity. Pakistan was not in collapse; it was managing conflict with calculated resolve.

## Media Management and Public Morale

In the high-stakes environment of Operation Bunyan-ul-Marsoos, where military precision and national defense took center stage, another front remained critical to Pakistan's success: media management and the preservation of public morale. While missiles and jets engaged the physical enemy, the battle for the hearts and minds of the Pakistani population played out in newsrooms, social media platforms, and living rooms across the country. At a time when misinformation could trigger panic and disunity, strategic communication and psychological resilience became as vital as battlefield tactics.

From the outset of the operation, Inter-Services Public Relations (ISPR)—the media wing of the Pakistan Armed Forces—took a commanding role in directing the national information campaign. The objective was clear: inform the public accurately, counter disinformation swiftly, and foster a spirit of unity and patriotism. Through pre-coordinated strategies, ISPR worked in close cooperation with the Ministry of Information, private media outlets, and digital content creators to ensure one consistent national voice.

### Timely, Transparent, and Controlled Messaging

ISPR's approach to media during the crisis was grounded in timely and factual communication, carefully designed to avoid both underreaction and sensationalism. Press briefings were scheduled regularly, with military spokespersons providing verified updates on the status of the conflict, areas affected, and the nature of Pakistan's response. This transparency helped the public feel informed rather than left in the dark, reducing the space for rumor-mongering.

Crucially, the tone of these communications struck a balance between calm reassurance and resolute strength. Rather than inciting hatred or hysteria, the messages emphasized the precision and restraint of Pakistan's actions, as well as its desire to avoid unnecessary escalation—fostering public confidence in leadership decisions.

**Mobilizing Private Media with National Responsibility**

Recognizing the immense influence of private media in shaping public perception, ISPR held high-level consultations with news executives, editors, and producers across major television networks and newspapers. Guidelines were shared on how to report responsibly during conflict, especially concerning footage from sensitive areas, speculation on targets, or operational details that could compromise national security.

Talk shows, which often veer toward divisive or sensational discussions, were encouraged to focus on analytical discourse, expert opinions, and unifying themes. Prominent defense analysts were given access to briefings to inform the public objectively. As a result, most major networks aligned themselves with a tone of calm strength, contributing to public morale rather than eroding it.

**Harnessing the Power of Social Media**

In today's digital era, social media often serves as the first source of news for the majority of citizens. Understanding its double-edged potential, ISPR expanded its digital presence during the operation through real-time updates, video footage of military readiness, and motivational content. Platforms such as Twitter, Facebook, YouTube, and Instagram were used strategically to counter fake news, block fear-inducing content, and share stories of heroism from the armed forces and the public.

Notably, trending hashtags like #StandWithPakistan, #BunyanUlMarsoos, and #SilentThunder created a sense of digital unity. The public was encouraged to share patriotic content, avoid unverified news, and report suspicious activity online—turning millions of ordinary citizens into active participants in the information defense of their country.

Meanwhile, cyber surveillance teams under the ISI monitored hostile propaganda, especially from foreign-based bots or accounts attempting to undermine Pakistani morale. Misinformation campaigns were identified and neutralized through fact-checking responses and coordinated digital takedowns in partnership with tech platforms.

**Psychological Support and Morale Building**

Beyond facts and updates, the media campaign focused on uplifting national spirit. Music videos, short films, interviews with soldiers and pilots, and emotional messages from the families of martyrs were broadcast widely. These were not mere propaganda—they resonated with an audience living under threat and looking for reassurance that their sacrifices were part of something noble and greater.

The campaign also featured religious and cultural figures who reminded the public of the historical resilience of the Pakistani people and the power of faith during trials. Imams spoke of the moral legitimacy of self-defense. Poets and artists contributed with creative expressions of solidarity. Sports personalities and celebrities posted messages of support for the armed forces, reinforcing national unity across generations and social strata.

**Media as a Unifying Force**

Perhaps most importantly, media during Operation Bunyan-ul-Marsoos did not become a tool for division or political gain. For once, networks and political commentators across the spectrum prioritized national interest over partisan narratives. This moment of solidarity in media tone and messaging played a significant role in ensuring that the nation stood united, not just against an external adversary, but also against the fear and anxiety that conflict inevitably brings.

# Chapter 8
# Global Eyes, Global Pressure

While fighter jets roared over contested skies and cyber units clashed in digital shadows, another critical battlefield emerged—the international diplomatic stage. Operation Bunyan-ul-Marsoos, though a regional military engagement, sent shockwaves across global corridors of power. With nuclear-armed neighbors locked in confrontation, the world watched anxiously, not just for its outcome, but for what it would mean for international peace, regional alliances, and great power balances.

In the immediate aftermath of the first air strikes, India rushed to shape the global narrative, portraying Pakistan's retaliatory campaign as escalatory aggression. New Delhi's envoys moved quickly in United Nations chambers and Western capitals, attempting to frame the events as justification for further diplomatic isolation of Pakistan. Yet, their arguments met a complex and cautious world order—one less inclined to take sides without scrutiny.

Pakistan, in contrast, activated a carefully prepared diplomatic response, coordinated by the Ministry of Foreign Affairs and strategic partners within the Organization of Islamic Cooperation (OIC). Leveraging intelligence briefings, preemptive engagement with allies, and appeals grounded in international law, Islamabad positioned itself as the party acting in self-defense under Article 51 of the UN Charter.

Meanwhile, the world's superpowers—the United States, China, and Russia—chose not to intervene directly but rather watched from the sidelines with measured silence. Their statements were carefully worded, reflecting a desire to avoid escalation while maintaining their strategic stakes in South Asia.

This chapter delves into the diplomatic maneuvers, strategic silence, and subtle alliances that shaped the international context of Bunyan-ul-Marsoos. As bombs fell and borders tensed, diplomacy became both the shield and the sword—determining not just what the world saw, but how it would remember this high-stakes confrontation.

## India's Diplomatic Moves at the UN

As the skies over South Asia lit up with the rumble of jet engines and the precision of airstrikes under Operation Bunyan-ul-Marsoos, India swiftly launched a parallel offensive—not in the air, but within the marble halls of the United Nations. Realizing the scale and symbolism of Pakistan's counteroffensive, New Delhi understood that the battlefield alone would not determine global perceptions. What followed was a strategically aggressive diplomatic campaign, aimed at framing Pakistan's military actions as unjustified, provocative, and dangerous for regional and global stability.

India's Permanent Mission to the UN in New York was immediately instructed to call for an emergency Security Council briefing, citing "cross-border escalation by Pakistan." At the same time, Indian envoys in Washington, London, Paris, and Canberra were directed to initiate high-level meetings with foreign ministries, urging them to issue statements of condemnation and caution. The tone was urgent, and the framing precise: Pakistan's strikes were not framed as retaliation, but rather as aggression against Indian sovereignty.

At the heart of India's diplomatic narrative were three primary claims:

1. Pakistan initiated a disproportionate escalation following an "isolated security incident," referring vaguely to the Pahalgam standoff.
2. Pakistan was harboring militant elements that continued to target Indian interests—a familiar and often-used narrative in post-2001 global politics.
3. India had the right to respond further, should the international community fail to restrain Pakistan.

This last point was particularly crucial. By implying that further strikes could occur, India was attempting to build a justification for extended military operations, should it choose to escalate again. It was a pre-emptive move to diplomatically sanitize potential future aggression.

## The Role of International Media and Public Opinion

India's diplomatic push was not limited to official channels. Simultaneously, its media diplomacy apparatus swung into action. Prominent Indian journalists, many of whom had long-standing ties with international outlets like The New York Times, BBC, Al Jazeera, and CNN, were provided with curated talking points, drone footage of alleged Pakistani positions, and interviews with Indian defense analysts. Articles and opinion pieces quickly began appearing, framing Pakistan's airstrikes as reckless and destabilizing.

India also tried to capitalize on existing global skepticism about Pakistan's counterterrorism efforts. Historical baggage was strategically revived, including references to the 2008 Mumbai attacks and the Pulwama bombing, to remind the international community of what India portrayed as "a pattern of destabilization." These references were not incidental—they were calculated attempts to turn the clock back and reintroduce older narratives under the new crisis.

## The Response at the United Nations

Despite the vigor of India's efforts, the UN Security Council (UNSC) responded with marked restraint. While discussions did take place behind closed doors, calls for an emergency session were met with silence or neutral stances by the five permanent members. China, a close ally of Pakistan, resisted any statement that painted Pakistan as the sole aggressor. Russia also urged both nations to de-escalate but refused to endorse India's version of events.

Even the UN Secretary-General's office issued only a generic statement, urging both countries to show restraint, resolve disputes diplomatically, and avoid civilian casualties. Crucially, the statement avoided assigning blame, signaling the international community's discomfort with India's attempt to singularly vilify Pakistan without accounting for the broader context of the conflict.

This diplomatic lukewarmness was a blow to India's expectations. New Delhi had hoped for an immediate wave of global condemnation against Pakistan, but what it received was diplomatic hedging and cautious neutrality.

**Quiet Pushback and Global Calculus**

Behind the scenes, several nations—especially those with strategic ties to both India and Pakistan—privately urged India to stand down. The United Arab Emirates, Saudi Arabia, and even France emphasized that while India had a right to self-defense, any further escalation could backfire diplomatically. Washington, while refraining from overt interference, advised both nations to pursue back-channel de-escalation.

India's claim that Pakistan had acted irrationally lost credibility when Pakistan released satellite imagery and operational data showing the surgical and restrained nature of its strikes. This transparency directly challenged India's narrative of "reckless aggression."

Moreover, countries in the Organization of Islamic Cooperation (OIC) largely sided with Pakistan, issuing statements that highlighted the "right of every sovereign nation to defend its territorial integrity." These developments undercut India's momentum, especially in the Global South.

# Pakistan's Allies and the OIC Response

In the aftermath of its precision counterstrikes under Operation Bunyan-ul-Marsoos, Pakistan understood that winning the diplomatic battle was as important as dominating the battlefield. As India attempted to portray Pakistan as the aggressor at the United Nations and in international media, Islamabad launched its own global outreach campaign—targeted, strategic, and deeply rooted in long-standing alliances, particularly within the Muslim world through the Organization of Islamic Cooperation (OIC).

While Pakistan's leadership had long recognized the importance of multilateral diplomacy, Bunyan-ul-Marsoos marked a new era of proactive engagement. Islamabad didn't wait to respond—it moved preemptively, ensuring that its allies were fully briefed before India could shape the global narrative unchallenged.

## Diplomatic Mobilization Across Muslim Capitals

In the first 24 hours after the initial wave of Pakistani airstrikes, Foreign Minister and senior diplomatic envoys were dispatched—or immediately connected via secure channels—to key OIC member states. Saudi Arabia, Turkey, the United Arab Emirates, Qatar, Iran, Malaysia, and Indonesia received detailed briefings supported by satellite imagery, timelines, and legal justifications.

The core message was direct: Pakistan had responded in self-defense under Article 51 of the UN Charter, and its military operations were carefully calibrated to avoid civilian targets, infrastructure, or unnecessary escalation.

Islamabad's approach to these allies was not rooted in emotional appeals or religious sentiment alone—it was rooted in mutual respect, shared security interests, and political realism. Pakistan emphasized that an Indian military doctrine rooted in pre-emptive strikes and unchallenged airspace dominance would set a dangerous precedent for all regional powers.

## The Organization of Islamic Cooperation: A Unified Voice

Perhaps the most decisive diplomatic win came in the form of a strong, unified response from the OIC. Within 72 hours of the operation, the OIC's General Secretariat issued a statement that not only acknowledged Pakistan's right to self-defense, but condemned India's initial escalation and urged New Delhi to cease actions that threatened regional peace.

This was followed by a joint resolution signed by over 40 OIC member states, affirming Pakistan's territorial integrity and supporting dialogue over conflict. The resolution specifically noted the need for international mediation in Kashmir and reiterated the OIC's historical stance on the right of self-determination for the Kashmiri people.

The timing and strength of this response dealt a blow to India's diplomatic campaign. While New Delhi had historically attempted to court certain Gulf nations through trade and defense ties, it became evident that OIC states were unwilling to forsake Pakistan in a time of perceived aggression.

## Bilateral Support and Strategic Messaging

Beyond multilateral forums, Pakistan also received strong bilateral support from key allies:

- **Turkey's President** issued a televised statement expressing "full support for Pakistan's right to protect its sovereignty," and offered to mediate between the two nations.
- **Malaysia** praised Pakistan's "measured and restrained" approach in contrast to what it called "unilateral provocations."
- **Iran**, while cautious due to its own regional concerns, acknowledged the legitimacy of self-defense and called for regional unity against destabilization.

Qatar and the UAE, though historically balanced in South Asian affairs, offered back-channel support by facilitating dialogue through diplomatic intermediaries and by refraining from endorsing India's stance despite heavy lobbying.

These diplomatic gestures were amplified by coordinated media appearances of Pakistani officials on Al Jazeera, TRT World, and Gulf-based media networks, ensuring that Pakistan's perspective was heard across millions of viewers in the Muslim world.

## The Power of Unity and Moral Legitimacy

The reason behind this wave of support wasn't just geopolitics—it was credibility. Pakistan's decision to respond militarily only after Indian provocation, its transparency with satellite and operational data, and its restraint in targeting military objectives only reinforced the global perception that it was acting as a responsible state in a difficult security environment.

Moreover, Pakistan's commitment to dialogue—even as its military forces remained on high alert—added moral weight to its diplomatic messaging. Islamabad consistently reiterated that it had no desire for war, only the need to preserve sovereignty and deter future aggression.

This stance resonated deeply across the Muslim world, particularly in countries with their own experiences of sovereignty threats and foreign intervention.

Pakistan's alliance-building and the OIC response during Operation Bunyan-ul-Marsoos showcased a masterclass in strategic diplomacy. At a moment when it could have been isolated or misunderstood, Pakistan turned its regional ties and religious unity into a formidable diplomatic shield. The widespread support not only blunted India's narrative but strengthened Pakistan's position as a nation that—despite immense provocation—acted with principle, precision, and purpose.

## US, China, and Russia: Silent Observers

While Pakistan and India exchanged strategic fire and launched diplomatic offensives, the global stage remained eerily silent—at least at the surface. The world's most powerful players—the United States, China, and Russia—chose to assume the role of silent observers, carefully analyzing the situation while refraining from overt involvement. Their silence, however, was not an indication of disinterest. Rather, it reflected a complex balancing act, as each superpower had deep-rooted strategic, economic, and military interests tied to both nations.

Their quiet posture was deliberate—a calculated silence, underscoring how geopolitical giants sometimes shape outcomes not through words, but through watchful restraint.

## United States: Balancing Act Between Allies

The United States found itself in an especially precarious position. On one hand, it viewed India as a key partner in its Indo-Pacific strategy and a counterweight to China's influence. On the other, it had a longstanding military and diplomatic relationship with Pakistan, especially in counterterrorism cooperation and Afghanistan.

In the early hours of Pakistan's Operation Bunyan-ul-Marsoos, Washington's response was limited to a cautious call for restraint. The U.S. State Department urged both nations to avoid further escalation and offered to assist with de-escalation talks if requested. Behind closed doors, however, the U.S. National Security Council (NSC) conducted emergency meetings, including high-level briefings from military attachés in Islamabad and New Delhi.

Sources suggest that while India privately pushed the U.S. for a statement condemning Pakistan's air strikes, American officials refused to endorse either side's version of events, citing the lack of independent verification. The U.S. Department of Defense, meanwhile, instructed its Central Command (CENTCOM) to monitor air and naval activities in the Arabian Sea, in case the conflict spilled over into broader maritime zones.

For Washington, the overriding concern was nuclear stability. Any direct alignment with India risked alienating Pakistan, potentially destabilizing the region and compromising U.S. strategic goals in the Middle East and Central Asia. Therefore, the U.S. chose diplomacy by silence, watching with vigilance and choosing words with surgical precision.

## China: The Strategic Patron of Restraint

China's silence was rooted in strategic necessity. As Pakistan's most enduring defense partner, and a country deeply invested in the China-Pakistan Economic Corridor (CPEC), China had every reason to be concerned about the escalation. But Beijing was also wary of antagonizing India too openly, particularly as tensions over Ladakh and the Line of Actual Control (LAC) remained unresolved.

When Indian diplomats attempted to garner Chinese condemnation of Pakistan's actions through indirect pressure in multilateral forums, Beijing resisted, issuing a brief and neutral statement urging "both parties to maintain peace and avoid further confrontation."

Behind the scenes, however, Chinese diplomats were in close contact with Islamabad. China's foreign minister spoke directly with Pakistan's leadership, reaffirming that Beijing supported Pakistan's right to territorial integrity and sovereignty. At the same time, China advised caution, encouraging Pakistan to avoid any actions that could lead to prolonged conflict or attract unnecessary international scrutiny.

There were also intelligence reports that Chinese satellites shared real-time battlefield imagery with Pakistan's military command, helping Islamabad verify Indian troop movements and air deployments. This silent support showcased China's commitment without diplomatic flamboyance—a style consistent with its "quiet strength" doctrine in South Asian affairs.

## Russia: Strategic Neutrality in Motion

Russia's position was the most complex of the three. Traditionally closer to India through defense deals and historical ties, Moscow had also steadily expanded relations with Pakistan in the fields of energy, military cooperation, and counterterrorism training.

In the face of Operation Bunyan-ul-Marsoos, Russia refused to take sides. Its Ministry of Foreign Affairs issued a short, carefully worded statement calling for "restraint, dialogue, and preservation of peace in South Asia." No reference was made to who escalated or retaliated first.

However, Russia's diplomatic silence did not mean inaction. Russian intelligence monitored the conflict closely, and officials at the Kremlin kept open lines of communication with both Islamabad and New Delhi. According to diplomatic leaks, Russia quietly warned India against provoking further military retaliation, fearing that any Indian misstep could pull Moscow into a wider diplomatic dilemma—especially as Russia was already embroiled in Eastern European conflicts and did not wish to see a new crisis develop on its eastern flank.

**Global Powers as Stabilizers, Not Arbiters**

Together, the strategic silence of the U.S., China, and Russia reflected a consensus—South Asia must not become a war theater. Their quiet stance was not a sign of disengagement, but a decision to avoid fanning the flames. Each power sought to act as a stabilizer, quietly influencing their respective allies behind closed doors while avoiding public commitments that could limit their maneuverability.

This delicate silence spoke volumes. It suggested that in a multipolar world, even the loudest actors sometimes choose quiet diplomacy over confrontation, and that the world's most powerful states understood the gravity of what was unfolding—opting to steady the balance rather than tip it.

# Chapter 9
# The Ceasefire Equation

After days of high-altitude dogfights, cyber interference, and coordinated strikes under Operation Bunyan-ul-Marsoos, the tempo of conflict slowed—not due to exhaustion, but through a deliberate recalibration on both sides. Beneath the surface of military tension and media speculation, diplomatic engines were quietly roaring. What emerged was a tense and fragile ceasefire, not publicly negotiated, but brokered through a web of international mediation, backchannel communications, and strategic calculation.

This chapter unpacks the anatomy of the ceasefire—how it came to be, what it meant, and what it did not. Despite no formal signing ceremony or joint announcement, a mutual decision to halt active operations reflected a turning point in the conflict's trajectory. It was a moment where symbolism gave way to pragmatism, and both Pakistan and India took a hard look at the limits of escalation.

Yet, the question lingered: Was the ceasefire a tactical pause orchestrated by master strategists, or a silent admission by both sides that further confrontation offered diminishing returns?

Behind this silence stood a coalition of quiet mediators. From Gulf states to Western capitals, private conversations, intelligence sharing, and subtle diplomatic nudges laid the foundation for de-escalation without embarrassment. The ceasefire allowed both countries to claim partial victories—India could say it had "contained aggression," while Pakistan could assert it had "re-established deterrence."

In this chapter, we explore the roles played by international actors, the psychological shift in both military doctrines, and the lessons internalized by both nations. More than just the end of hostilities, the ceasefire represented a complex equation of deterrence, diplomacy, and unspoken agreements that reshaped South Asia's strategic landscape—at least, until the next spark.

## International Mediation Behind the Curtain

While missiles fell silent and jet engines cooled, the world took a breath—but not without effort. The ceasefire that concluded the high-stakes clash during Operation Bunyan-ul-Marsoos was not merely a product of military exhaustion or coincidence. It was the result of intense, layered, and discreet international mediation efforts, carried out behind closed doors and off the headlines. This was diplomacy in its most subtle and potent form—quiet channels, unacknowledged intermediaries, and carefully crafted pressure points.

Though neither Pakistan nor India publicly admitted to outside influence, multiple sources across diplomatic circles later confirmed that a select group of global actors intervened decisively to halt the slide toward full-scale war.

## The Gulf Nexus: Silent Influencers

The Gulf region, particularly Saudi Arabia and the United Arab Emirates, played a key mediating role during the peak of the escalation. Both countries maintained strong economic and political ties with New Delhi, while also having historical, religious, and strategic solidarity with Islamabad. With vast South Asian diasporas residing in their borders, they had a vested interest in ensuring stability between the two nuclear-armed neighbors.

According to intelligence leaks and diplomatic reporting, it was the Crown Prince of Saudi Arabia who first initiated personal phone calls to both Prime Ministers. These were not ceremonial gestures. The calls conveyed clear concerns about the regional ripple effects of the conflict, oil market instability, and the danger to millions of expatriate workers. The message was simple: resolve this, or we will be forced to recalibrate our relations.

The UAE followed suit, dispatching high-level envoys to both capitals. These diplomats brought offers of indirect communication, relaying positions, clarifying demands, and eventually laying the groundwork for what became the undeclared truce.

## Washington's Whisper Diplomacy

Though the United States refrained from overt alignment, Washington's role was crucial in shaping the ceasefire. The U.S. National Security Council (NSC), in coordination with the Pentagon and Department of State, launched what insiders called a "whisper campaign of restraint." This involved unofficial messages, relayed through ambassadors, military attachés, and trusted former diplomats.

Pakistan was assured that its right to self-defense had been noted and understood by the international community. Meanwhile, India was warned—subtly but unmistakably—that any further escalation might harm its image as a responsible regional power and jeopardize ongoing defense and tech deals.

More significantly, the U.S. urged both nations to "leave space for diplomacy" by pausing operations and refraining from further provocations. The implicit threat of international sanctions or a freeze on arms sales remained unspoken but understood.

**China's Strategic Signals**

China, Pakistan's all-weather ally, maintained its usual low-key but firm approach. While Beijing did not directly broker talks, it issued targeted diplomatic warnings to New Delhi through backdoor military and political channels. These messages conveyed that any strike threatening Pakistan's core defense infrastructure might trigger Chinese logistical and intelligence involvement, escalating the conflict unpredictably.

At the same time, China encouraged Pakistan to maintain restraint and avoid symbolic overreach. In doing so, it helped anchor Pakistan's diplomatic posture as one grounded in defense, not offense.

Behind the scenes, Chinese diplomats engaged with Gulf states, Russia, and even the European Union to build consensus around de-escalation. Their goal was clear: prevent South Asia from becoming a broader geopolitical flashpoint that could disrupt global economic and security frameworks.

## Russia and the European Middle Ground

Russia, traditionally aligned with India but increasingly connected with Pakistan through defense and energy ties, acted as a quiet balancer. Moscow's approach was to facilitate indirect communication without taking sides. It quietly offered its good offices for potential peace talks and shared neutral intelligence assessments with both nations.

Simultaneously, several European states, particularly France and Germany, contributed by applying normative pressure through diplomatic channels. Their message emphasized that both countries risked reputational damage and economic fallout if the situation spiraled.

France, a major arms supplier to India, also reminded New Delhi of its obligations under international humanitarian law, cautioning against disproportionate military responses.

## Unseen Brokers, Visible Impact

It is often said that the most effective diplomacy is the kind that never makes headlines. This was precisely the nature of the ceasefire that emerged from Operation Bunyan-ul-Marsoos. There were no televised summits, no historic handshakes. What there was, instead, were trusted relationships, candid assessments, and coordinated restraint.

Each international actor played their part not by imposing decisions, but by offering off-ramps, creating space for face-saving, and reminding both nations of the consequences of unchecked escalation. In effect, they constructed a corridor of silence in which both militaries could step back without appearing weak.

In summary, the ceasefire equation was not just a military or political decision—it was a diplomatic triumph conducted in shadows. From Riyadh to Washington, from Beijing to Paris, the world's centers of power aligned briefly to stabilize a volatile region. And while neither Islamabad nor New Delhi publicly acknowledged the mediation, their decision to pause spoke volumes. In diplomacy, what is left unsaid often carries the most weight.

## Strategic Pause: Calculated or Conceded?

The abrupt cessation of hostilities following the Pakistani-led Operation Bunyan-ul-Marsoos left the international community and regional analysts asking a critical question: was the pause in conflict a strategic calculation, or a reluctant concession forced by external and internal pressures? The answer, as with most events in geopolitical warfare, lies in a nuanced understanding of timing, objectives, and silent negotiations.

**The Military Equation**

From a military standpoint, the pause came at a moment when both countries had demonstrated their capabilities. Pakistan's air strikes, conducted with surgical precision, had penetrated deep into Indian airspace, hitting symbolic and strategic targets without triggering widespread civilian casualties. India's initial offensive had already been met with equal—if not superior—force. With both air forces on high alert and air defense systems fully activated, any further escalation risked leading to a widening of the battlefield and massive casualties.

For Pakistan, continuing the offensive after restoring deterrence could risk overextending operational success and appearing aggressive, thereby weakening its diplomatic position. Choosing to pause solidified its narrative as a state that acts with restraint and responsibility, even when provoked. Within the armed forces' strategic circles, this was not seen as a climb-down but as mission accomplished—objectives achieved, capabilities demonstrated, and deterrence re-established.

For India, a continuation of the conflict after being hit on critical bases such as Pathankot and BrahMos storage sites would have likely exposed further vulnerabilities in its air defense and intelligence coordination. The operational momentum had tilted, and pushing forward would have entailed both military and political risks—particularly with public sentiment teetering between nationalist fervor and growing anxiety.

**Political Optics and Domestic Considerations**

In democracies and military-influenced states alike, optics matter. Both governments had to ensure that their actions were digestible for domestic audiences. In India, the initial narrative of "surgical strikes" and a tough posture against Pakistan had galvanized public support. However, once Pakistan responded with comparable if not superior effectiveness, the government had to reassess whether continued conflict would generate support or political backlash.

Pakistan, on the other hand, had rallied domestic unity. The mission had boosted morale, restored pride after years of asymmetric pressures, and exhibited the nation's military maturity. The government's message was clear: we do not seek war, but we are prepared for it. By halting operations voluntarily, Pakistan elevated its diplomatic standing—both at home and abroad.

## International Signals and Strategic Deterrence

A key element that shaped the pause was the message sent to the global powers. Pakistan's restraint despite military advantage was seen as a marker of responsibility. This undermined India's attempts to portray Pakistan as a reckless actor. By stepping back after proving its capacity, Pakistan positioned itself as a regional power capable of restraint, even under duress.

India, meanwhile, received subtle but firm signals from global allies and trade partners, especially the U.S. and European nations, urging de-escalation. In a globalized economy, conflict affects markets, energy flows, and international confidence. The silence from Washington, Moscow, and Beijing was not passive—it was strategic. Their quiet watchfulness conveyed a clear message: end this before it spirals.

This indirect pressure reinforced the logic of a pause—not as a concession, but as a necessary recalibration within a globalized, nuclear-capable context.

## Lessons from Limited War

The concept of "limited war" between nuclear states is inherently paradoxical. There is only so far escalation can go before it crosses thresholds no nation wants to confront. The strategic pause reinforced this reality. It demonstrated that modern warfare, especially between nuclear-armed rivals, has boundaries, and crossing them invites uncontrollable consequences.

Both Pakistan and India walked up to the edge of those boundaries—but did not cross them. This in itself was a lesson in strategic signaling, where actions are choreographed not just for immediate gain, but for long-term equilibrium.

Pakistan's leadership, both civilian and military, understood that the narrative of strength is better sustained by choosing when to stop, not just when to strike. And India, despite its initial aggressive posture, realized that absorbing blows while retaining control over escalation could serve its long-term strategic positioning.

**A Calculated Endgame**

In the final analysis, the cessation of active hostilities was a joint, calculated decision shaped by military, political, and diplomatic variables. It was neither a victory cry nor a white flag. It was the recognition that each side had tested the other, measured the risks, and opted for containment over catastrophe.

While the ceasefire may appear sudden, it was the culmination of days of strategic deliberation, international communication, and internal reassessment. Both nations paused not out of weakness, but out of recognition that modern conflict, particularly in South Asia, is not merely a matter of battlefield wins—but of narrative control, diplomatic strength, and long-term deterrence.

## Messages Sent, Lessons Learned

The conclusion of hostilities under Operation Bunyan-ul-Marsoos left more than just a ceasefire line—it left behind a trail of unspoken but deeply understood messages, etched into the memory of both nations and observers around the world. As the dust settled, analysts and policymakers began dissecting the conflict not just for what was done, but for what it signified, what was learned, and how future engagements would be shaped by this historic confrontation.

This section explores the strategic messages delivered by both sides, the regional and global lessons extracted from the operation, and the new doctrines likely to emerge in its wake.

**Pakistan's Message: We Are No Longer Reactive**

Perhaps the most defining message Pakistan delivered through Bunyan-ul-Marsoos was that it would no longer accept preemptive aggression silently. For decades, Pakistan had been accused of strategic ambiguity—responding too late or not at all to provocations, relying on nuclear deterrence as its only shield. This mission shattered that perception.

With coordinated airstrikes deep into Indian territory, Pakistan demonstrated that its conventional military strength had matured into a technologically capable, strategically disciplined force. The strikes were not reckless; they were symbolic, accurate, and intentionally restrained—avoiding civilian casualties while exposing India's vulnerabilities. This underscored a new doctrine: credible conventional deterrence backed by readiness, not just rhetoric.

Additionally, Pakistan made clear that its response would be multi-domain. From cyber warfare and electronic jamming to strategic media messaging and diplomatic positioning, Islamabad flexed its muscles on every front—military, psychological, and informational.

**India's Message: Escalation Has a Ceiling**

India's conduct during the crisis, though initially aggressive, revealed certain limits. After facing Pakistan's air response and cyber tactics, India refrained from further escalation. The subtext was clear: India, despite its larger military and international partnerships, recognized that open war with Pakistan would come at a heavy cost, both economically and diplomatically.

This conveyed an important message—not of weakness, but of strategic restraint informed by hard realities. The Indian government may have hoped to assert dominance through early shows of force, but the counterblows from Pakistan forced a recalibration.

The limited scope of India's subsequent actions signaled to its adversaries and allies alike that New Delhi does not seek prolonged confrontation, especially when faced with calibrated and precise retaliation. While maintaining a tough domestic narrative, India simultaneously conveyed to international powers that it would not jeopardize regional stability or global economic interests for symbolic military gains.

**Regional Lessons: The New Face of South Asian Conflict**

One of the clearest lessons drawn from the conflict is that South Asian military doctrines have evolved. The use of drones, satellite-guided munitions, real-time battlefield coordination, and hybrid operations—such as cyberattacks and information warfare—marked a departure from traditional battlefield encounters.

Both India and Pakistan displayed unprecedented military agility, with operations planned and executed in days rather than weeks. This has introduced new risks for crisis management: the speed at which events escalated left little room for traditional diplomacy to intervene early. The region now faces an era where conflict escalation can move from provocation to retaliation in hours, increasing the chances of miscalculation.

Additionally, the conflict showcased the importance of public morale and perception warfare. Control over narrative—both domestically and internationally—became as important as control over the skies. Governments realized that information is not just power, but a form of weaponry.

**Global Lessons: Silence Doesn't Mean Inaction**

Another key takeaway was the role of global powers. The United States, China, and Russia chose strategic silence, but were deeply involved through backchannel diplomacy. This affirmed a new form of crisis mediation—informal, fast-moving, and confidential—operating in contrast to traditional summits or UN sessions.

International actors sent a clear message: they will not publicly arbitrate South Asian conflicts, but will influence outcomes behind the scenes. Their goal is containment, not confrontation, and any state that ignores this unspoken consensus risks isolation or sanctions.

Furthermore, Middle Eastern players emerged as unexpected stabilizers. Saudi Arabia and the UAE demonstrated their capacity to mediate with credibility on both sides, suggesting a future where regional power brokers—not just Western capitals—play roles in preventing war.

**Doctrine Redefined: From Deterrence to Deterrence-Plus**

The greatest strategic lesson of all may be doctrinal. Both India and Pakistan learned that deterrence today must be layered. It cannot rely solely on nuclear thresholds or conventional superiority. The new model is "Deterrence-Plus"—a synthesis of rapid response capabilities, global media control, cyber warfare, and precise targeting.

For Pakistan, this doctrine elevated its military credibility and demonstrated its ability to achieve military and diplomatic objectives without triggering full-scale war. For India, it served as a reminder that modern conflict is about adaptability, not just armament.

Bunyan-ul-Marsoos was not just a military operation—it was a message. It said to the region and the world: South Asia's future conflicts will not be slow-moving, predictable affairs. They will be sharp, fast, and fought on many fronts. The challenge now lies in ensuring that the lessons learned from this moment are applied—so the next chapter doesn't begin with missiles, but with meaningful dialogue.

# Chapter 10
# Youm-e-Tashakur: A Nation Honors

In the aftermath of Operation Bunyan-ul-Marsoos, as the echoes of jet engines faded and the airwaves cleared of war rhetoric, Pakistan paused—not in silence, but in solemn gratitude. On May 16, the government officially declared Youm-e-Tashakur, a Day of Gratitude, to honor those who stood tall in the defense of the nation. This was not merely a ceremonial event; it was a collective expression of pride, reverence, and national unity, marking a rare moment where the military, civilian population, and state institutions stood as one.

The chapter delves into the symbolic and emotional significance of this national observance. Streets were lined with flags, homes glowed with green lights, and the air was thick with stories of valor. Schools held special assemblies, mosques offered prayers for martyrs and veterans, and media channels aired tributes to those who made victory possible—both in the skies and on the ground.

But beyond the spectacle lay deeper narratives: the unspoken sacrifices of pilots who flew into danger, the tireless endurance of ground crews who kept machines ready through sleepless nights, and the unwavering resolve of commanders who made fateful decisions.

Youm-e-Tashakur became more than a calendar date. It became a symbol of a nation's resilience, a moment when gratitude turned into remembrance, and remembrance into resolve. In this final chapter, we reflect on the human spirit that powered Pakistan's defense—the faces behind the mission, the stories often untold, and the honors that sought to immortalize them.

## May 16 Declared Day of Gratitude

When the dust settled after the tense standoff of Operation Bunyan-ul-Marsoos, Pakistan's leadership recognized the moment not merely as a military accomplishment but as a historic triumph of unity, resolve, and disciplined strength. To commemorate this moment, the government declared May 16 as Youm-e-Tashakur—a Day of Gratitude. This date was selected to immortalize the day when hostilities ceased and the nation emerged with dignity intact, its sovereignty defended, and its people united like never before.

The announcement came directly from the Prime Minister's Office. It was broadcast live on all major television networks, accompanied by visuals of flag-raising ceremonies, jets in formation, and a national anthem echoing across the country. In his address to the nation, the Prime Minister stated, "This day is not just a celebration of military success, but a tribute to the spirit of our people, the precision of our armed forces, and the will of a sovereign nation that stood tall in the face of aggression."

## National Commemoration Across the Country

From the mountainous outposts of Siachen to the coastal bases in Gwadar, Pakistan's landscape transformed overnight. Government buildings were adorned with national flags and banners bearing messages of thanks and remembrance. Schools, colleges, and universities organized special programs where students recited poems, performed skits, and shared stories of bravery drawn from the recent operation.

Mosques across the country held special duas (prayers) for martyrs, veterans, and their families. Church groups, temples, and gurdwaras also participated, illustrating a rare display of interfaith unity on a national level. It was a day where political divisions were set aside, and citizens came together under a single flag.

In major cities like Islamabad, Lahore, Karachi, and Peshawar, military parades and aerial flypasts thrilled onlookers. Fighter jets flew in formation, and skydivers descended carrying massive national flags, landing to roaring applause. The public thronged the streets, waving flags, singing national songs, and embracing the soldiers who returned from their missions.

## Media's Role in Shaping the Narrative

Television and digital platforms played a central role in shaping the memory and meaning of Youm-e-Tashakur. For 24 hours, news channels broadcast documentaries, interviews with pilots, and behind-the-scenes footage of the mission. Special tributes aired featuring the families of those who served, often showing mothers speaking proudly of their sons in uniform, and children beaming with pride as they spoke of their fathers' heroism.

Documentaries narrated by famous artists revisited the timeline of the operation, showcasing the professionalism of the Pakistan Air Force, the coordination between the three services, and the country's dignified approach to retaliation. Music videos dedicated to fallen heroes went viral on social media, with hashtags like #YoumeTashakur, #SilentThunder, and #BunyanulMarsoos trending across all platforms.

## A Moment of Reflection and Unity

Perhaps the most profound impact of Youm-e-Tashakur was the introspection it sparked among the Pakistani people. For once, the focus was not just on defeating an adversary, but on honoring discipline, integrity, and national purpose. Across drawing rooms, cafes, and classrooms, people spoke less of war and more of what it means to stand united. Veterans were invited to schools and offices to share their experiences, and families of servicemen were publicly acknowledged for their sacrifices.

In rural towns and urban centers alike, the message was consistent: this day was not for jingoism, but for gratitude—for peace, for protection, and for principles upheld in adversity.

## Institutionalization of the Day

The government announced that May 16 would be formally added to the national calendar as an annual observance, with plans to introduce educational content related to the operation in school syllabi. Museums began curating special exhibits on Operation Bunyan-ul-Marsoos, displaying flight suits, mission maps, and letters exchanged between commanders and their families.

A dedicated monument titled "The Thunder of Gratitude" was commissioned to be built in Islamabad, symbolizing the unity of armed forces and the resilience of the people. The monument would feature a sculpture of interlocked hands—representing military and civilian solidarity—etched with the names of the operation's key contributors.

**Legacy Beyond Celebration**

More than anything, May 16 became a date etched into the emotional DNA of Pakistan. It was no longer just about fighter jets or radar signatures. It became a symbol of what the nation could achieve when its institutions aligned, when its people believed, and when its response was shaped by faith, not fury.

This day served as a reminder that Pakistan, often tested but never broken, has within it a core of unshakable resolve. The gratitude expressed was not only for the heroes in uniform but also for the doctors who stood ready, the engineers who maintained systems under fire, the families who waited silently, and the civilians who remained calm under threat.

## Stories of Pilots and Ground Heroes

Behind every successful military operation lies a network of brave individuals whose stories often remain untold. During Operation Bunyan-ul-Marsoos, the Pakistan Air Force and supporting ground units showcased not only tactical precision but also human courage, resilience, and sacrifice. From fighter pilots soaring into hostile airspace to technicians working under blackout conditions, each played a crucial role. This chapter pays tribute to those silent warriors whose actions defined the mission and inspired a nation.

## Squadron Leader Taimoor Khan: The Falcon of Sargodha

One of the most celebrated heroes of the operation was Squadron Leader Taimoor Khan, a seasoned F-16 pilot stationed at the Sargodha airbase. Known for his sharp instincts and calm under pressure, Taimoor was selected to lead the retaliatory strike on an Indian forward radar installation. The mission was high-risk—Indian radar systems were partially functional, and anti-air defenses were reportedly on alert.

Flying low to avoid detection, Taimoor and his wingman executed a precise strike within the assigned window. His F-16 released smart munitions that disabled the target, ensuring minimal collateral damage. Taimoor's aircraft was briefly locked by an Indian surface-to-air missile system, but his evasive maneuvering and electronic countermeasures allowed him to escape unscathed. He landed to a standing ovation from ground crews and was later hailed as the "Falcon of Sargodha."

## Flight Lieutenant Naila Qureshi: Eyes in the Sky

While fighter pilots received much of the limelight, the mission would not have been possible without the unmanned aerial surveillance teams. Flight Lieutenant Naila Qureshi, one of the few female officers in the drone command unit, led a critical reconnaissance operation using indigenous UAVs to monitor Indian troop and radar movement before the main strike.

Working 36 hours without proper rest, she and her team tracked real-time heat signatures of Indian convoys and verified the shutdown of BrahMos missile sites. Her efforts ensured that Pakistani jets had up-to-date intel during their operations. Though she never left the ground, her accuracy in targeting data directly contributed to mission success. She became a symbol of dedication and inclusion, inspiring thousands of young women across the country.

### Chief Technician Riaz Mehmood: The Unsung Engineer

Fighter jets are only as good as the teams that keep them flying. At the Kamra airbase, Chief Technician Riaz Mehmood led a team of engineers responsible for maintaining a squadron of JF-17 Thunders. During the operation, one jet returned with hydraulic failure—a critical issue that, if unresolved, would have grounded it for days.

Working through the night in blackout conditions—where even a flashlight could compromise location security—Riaz and his team rebuilt the system from scratch, using salvaged components and manual calibration tools. By morning, the jet was operational and ready for its next sortie.

Riaz didn't wear a flight suit, but his contribution was acknowledged when his unit was awarded a special citation for technical excellence. His story became a lesson in how heroism doesn't always require a cockpit—it requires commitment.

### Ground Security Units: Shielding the Backbone

While jets dominated the skies, ground security personnel secured runways, radars, and command centers from potential sabotage or enemy strikes. At an undisclosed airbase near Bahawalpur, a group of airmen intercepted and neutralized a hostile surveillance drone believed to be mapping the airfield for a potential attack.

The mission required both rapid reaction and cool-headed analysis. With no external support, the team tracked the drone using thermal scopes and shot it down using anti-drone rifles—a rarely used but highly specialized piece of equipment. Their vigilance likely prevented preemptive strikes on aircraft hangars and refueling stations.

## Voices from the Families

The human side of these stories extends to the families waiting back home. In a widely circulated interview, Mrs. Farzana Taimoor, wife of Squadron Leader Taimoor, shared how their three children were unaware of the dangers their father faced. "I prayed every night that I wouldn't have to explain why their father didn't come back," she said, tears in her eyes. "And when he did, I told them he had gone to protect the skies so they could sleep peacefully."

The courage of these families, the silent sacrifices of spouses and parents, became an invisible but powerful force that held the home front together.

## Commemorating the Heroes

Following the operation, many of these individuals received national awards and gallantry medals. Taimoor Khan was awarded the Sitara-e-Jurat, Naila Qureshi received the Tamgha-e-Basalat, and Chief Technician Riaz was given a Presidential Commendation. Their stories were added to military training curriculums as examples of exemplary service.

Yet, for many of them, the medals mattered less than the knowledge that their actions contributed to national honor and peace.

# Military Honors and National Awards

In the aftermath of Operation Bunyan-ul-Marsoos, the Pakistani state found itself in a rare moment of unity and clarity—grateful, proud, and determined to honor those who had made the impossible look effortless. The military success of the operation did not just come from cutting-edge technology or battle-hardened strategies; it came from human beings who performed under pressure, served in silence, and stood unwavering in the face of adversity.

Recognizing these sacrifices and acts of excellence, the Government of Pakistan, in coordination with the Armed Forces, announced a historic round of military honors and national awards, aimed at acknowledging heroism across all tiers—from frontline pilots to intelligence operatives, from logistics technicians to drone analysts.

## A National Ceremony of Recognition

The formal awards ceremony was held at Aiwan-e-Sadr (The President's House) in Islamabad on July 14, exactly two months after Youm-e-Tashakur. It was broadcast live across the country, with military bands playing national melodies and an audience comprising decorated officers, their families, civilian leadership, and dignitaries from allied nations.

President of Pakistan, in his role as Commander-in-Chief, presided over the honors, while the Chiefs of Army, Navy, and Air Force stood side-by-side in a powerful display of joint leadership. In his keynote address, the President remarked, "Today, we do not merely pin medals on uniforms. We celebrate the soul of Pakistan—

the resolve, the courage, the unity that shines brightest in times of darkness."

## Gallantry Awards for Combat Heroes

Among the highest honors awarded was the Sitara-e-Jurat (Star of Courage), conferred upon Squadron Leader Taimoor Khan, whose deep penetration strike on an Indian radar facility became the tactical fulcrum of the operation. His daring maneuver under hostile air defense radar, and his precise targeting, saved countless lives and earned him a permanent place in the history of aerial warfare.

Another notable recipient was Wing Commander Rafiq Mehsud, who led the suppression of Indian S-400 air defense installations with electronic jamming coordination. His real-time communication with airborne assets ensured the mission's success. He received the Tamgha-e-Jurat, acknowledging his role in neutralizing a major threat.

Posthumously, Flight Officer Bilal Haroon, who perished in a technical crash while returning from a reconnaissance mission, was awarded the Sitara-e-Basalat. His widow and young son received the medal in a moment that moved the entire nation. It reminded everyone that some heroes never return to hear the applause.

## Honors for Technical and Ground Support

Recognizing that missions are never carried by pilots alone, the military extended high honors to technicians and engineers. Chief Technician Riaz Mehmood, celebrated for restoring a damaged JF-17 Thunder in less than 12 hours using improvised repairs, was awarded the Tamgha-e-Khidmat (Medal of Service).

Flight Lieutenant Naila Qureshi, who headed real-time drone surveillance and target mapping, received the Tamgha-e-Basalat. Her gender and age—being one of the youngest awardees—became a symbol of inclusiveness and evolution within the ranks. She represented the growing role of women in defense beyond traditional barriers.

### ISI and Intelligence Community Recognition

For the first time in many years, civilian intelligence officers working alongside military units were publicly acknowledged. Although their identities were kept classified, a group of 13 officers from ISI and MI received closed-door commendations for actionable intelligence that helped prevent Indian missile strikes on Pakistani airfields.

Additionally, the Director of Strategic Communications, responsible for countering Indian media narratives and shaping international perception, was awarded the Sitara-e-Imtiaz (Civil) for excellence in information warfare.

### Civilian Participation and Special Awards

In a powerful gesture, the government extended recognition beyond uniformed personnel. Awards were also given to civilian volunteers and private sector contributors. Engineers from the National Radio & Telecommunication Corporation (NRTC), who rapidly developed signal scramblers, were awarded Presidential Commendations.

Even local communities near airbases were honored. In Chakwal, villagers helped military security forces intercept a suspicious vehicle near an ammunition depot. The village elders were brought to Islamabad and publicly thanked for their vigilance, underscoring that national defense is a shared responsibility.

**A Monumental Legacy**

These awards were not only medals of honor—they were instruments of legacy-building. Their recipients were added to official military history, and their acts became case studies for training future cadets and officers.

In schools, students began writing essays about these heroes. In homes, parents told their children stories of bravery that happened not on distant fronts, but in their own skies. The heroes of Bunyan-ul-Marsoos were not faceless shadows—they were brothers, sisters, mentors, and neighbors.

The military honors and national awards issued after Operation Bunyan-ul-Marsoos represented something far greater than ceremony. They reflected a nation's appreciation for excellence in duty, clarity in purpose, and courage under fire. These awards told the world—and future generations—that when Pakistan is tested, it responds not with chaos, but with discipline, unity, and enduring honor.

# Chapter 11
# Psychological & Military Impact

Operation Bunyan-ul-Marsoos did more than deliver strategic military responses; it reshaped perceptions, shifted doctrines, and sent shockwaves through the psychological fabric of both the region and the international stage. For the first time in decades, the balance of power in South Asia was not just questioned—it was recalibrated in the minds of military planners, political analysts, and ordinary citizens alike.

Pakistan's calibrated and disciplined display of force served as a reassertion of deterrence—a signal that any aggression would be met with precise and proportionate retaliation. This was not a message delivered through fiery speeches, but through tactical airstrikes, electronic warfare, and information dominance. The mission reignited discussions on how deterrence in South Asia functions in the modern era—beyond nuclear posturing and conventional saber-rattling.

At the same time, the psychological impact on India was significant. The operation exposed vulnerabilities and forced a reckoning within India's military, media, and political establishments. Narratives of invincibility were challenged. Political leadership faced criticism over intelligence failures and miscalculated provocations, while the public's perception of national security underwent a dramatic shift.

Globally, the operation triggered a reassessment of South Asia's strategic dynamics. Major powers took note—not just of the firepower displayed—but of the maturity with which Pakistan executed its mission. Think tanks, intelligence agencies, and foreign ministries reevaluated risk models, diplomatic strategies, and alliance considerations in the region.

This chapter delves into the mental and strategic aftermath of the operation, dissecting how Pakistan's restraint, precision, and narrative control created a lasting impact on military doctrines, political discourse, and global diplomacy. In doing so, it reveals that the most enduring victories are often not won on the battlefield—but in the hearts, minds, and policies shaped thereafter.

## A Doctrine of Deterrence Reasserted

The events of Operation Bunyan-ul-Marsoos did not merely respond to provocation—they strategically recalibrated Pakistan's deterrence doctrine. For decades, South Asia's security calculus rested precariously on a thin thread of assumed balances. India's growing conventional edge, bolstered by advanced missile systems, air defense networks, and international alliances, had emboldened a belief in uncontested escalation. That perception was shattered not with nuclear threats, but with precision, professionalism, and psychological strength.

Historically, Pakistan's deterrence doctrine has been anchored in minimum credible deterrence, especially within the nuclear spectrum. However, the evolution of hybrid warfare, surgical strikes, and cross-border skirmishes demanded a more dynamic, layered approach. Bunyan-ul-Marsoos became the embodiment of that shift: a message that Pakistan's deterrence was not theoretical—it was active, responsive, and adaptive.

At the heart of this reassertion was clarity of intent without recklessness. Pakistan did not launch unprovoked attacks, nor did it respond with uncalculated rage. Instead, it delivered limited, proportionate, yet surgically precise strikes—targets were carefully chosen to minimize civilian casualties while inflicting significant strategic and symbolic damage on India's military infrastructure. This deliberate approach communicated strength, not desperation. It displayed discipline, not fragility.

This redefined deterrence, proving it is not solely about possessing destructive capability, but about demonstrating the will and skill to use force responsibly when red lines are crossed. In doing so, Pakistan reinforced the credibility of its red lines—not only to India, but to global observers who often viewed the region through a lens of irrationality and unpredictability.

One key element was the operational secrecy and surprise. Indian defenses, including the much-touted S-400 air defense system and BrahMos missile sites, were left vulnerable despite their technological superiority. By evading these systems and striking with precision, Pakistan revealed the limitations of overconfidence in hardware alone, and elevated the value of doctrine, strategy, and agility. The balance of deterrence had been adjusted—not through parity in numbers, but through superiority in tactical judgment.

Another vital component was the non-nuclear messaging. Pakistan's response stayed well within conventional bounds. It did not evoke nuclear posturing or engage in rhetoric suggesting catastrophic retaliation. This restraint made the deterrence more acceptable internationally, reinforcing the image of Pakistan as a responsible actor capable of measured, sovereign defense, rather than impulsive aggression. The international community, including key states like China, the U.S., and Russia, observed this nuance and recalibrated their regional risk perceptions accordingly.

Internally, this operation also had a powerful psychological deterrent effect. The success restored public confidence in the nation's defense institutions and generated an atmosphere of national pride without warmongering. It signaled to adversaries that the Pakistani military was battle-ready, deeply integrated across branches, and no longer reactive but proactively calibrated. This internal morale boost is a silent but powerful force multiplier in sustaining deterrence over time.

Furthermore, electronic warfare (EW) and cyber capabilities demonstrated during the mission opened a new frontier in the deterrence matrix. Disruptions in Indian radar communications, the jamming of targeting systems, and psychological operations through digital platforms emphasized that modern deterrence must span multiple domains—land, air, space, and cyberspace. This multidimensional capacity marked a doctrinal evolution for Pakistan, showing it was no longer bound to traditional definitions of battlefield superiority.

Finally, the naming of the operation—"Bunyan-ul-Marsoos," meaning "a wall made of solid cemented ranks" (Qur'an 61:4)—played a crucial role in deterrence psychology. It connected strategic defense with ideological unity. In an environment where perception often precedes action, this choice of name and the spiritual framework it invoked fostered both national cohesion and moral legitimacy. It portrayed Pakistan's defense not just as military necessity, but as a duty embraced by a unified, principled society.

In the post-operation analysis conducted by think tanks and military colleges across the globe, the common consensus was clear: Pakistan had effectively redefined deterrence for the 21st century. It proved that a smaller but more integrated, mission-oriented force with a clear doctrine can not only counter a conventionally superior opponent, but also influence strategic thinking on both sides of the border.

In essence, "A Doctrine of Deterrence Reasserted" was not just a lesson for India—it became a case study for modern military strategy in asymmetrical power environments. It reminded the world that deterrence lives not in weapons alone, but in the clarity of a nation's resolve, the precision of its response, and the maturity of its restraint.

## Indian Media and Political Fallout

Operation Bunyan-ul-Marsoos not only stunned Indian defense establishments but also sent tremors through its political and media ecosystems. For a country where national pride and regional dominance are deeply interwoven with public narratives, the psychological aftershocks of Pakistan's precise and disciplined military action were far-reaching. Indian media, political parties, and military analysts scrambled to control the narrative—only to find themselves entangled in contradictions, internal criticism, and a loss of strategic face.

**The Narrative Unravels**

In the hours following Pakistan's retaliatory strikes, Indian media, initially confident and aggressive in tone, shifted rapidly into a state of confusion and contradiction. Early broadcasts claimed "minimal impact," suggesting that Pakistan's strikes had "missed all critical targets." However, as satellite images and independent analyses began surfacing—particularly through international platforms—those claims fell apart.

Reputable global outlets published clear imagery showing damage to Indian radar facilities and support infrastructure near forward airbases. Former military officials, once used as media pundits to project dominance, were forced to acknowledge the vulnerability of Indian installations and the failure to intercept Pakistani jets despite the presence of S-400 systems and other sophisticated equipment.

In the face of growing public scrutiny, Indian defense spokespersons provided vague and inconsistent briefings. The disconnect between official statements and media coverage created a credibility vacuum, one that was quickly filled with online memes, satire, and frustration from Indian citizens who had expected retaliation or, at the very least, a clearer official response.

**Political Blame Games and Internal Pressure**

With general elections on the horizon, the political cost of the perceived military failure became evident. Opposition parties seized the opportunity to criticize the ruling government for what they labeled as a "reckless gamble" that led to unnecessary escalation and exposure of Indian vulnerabilities.

A prominent member of the opposition remarked in Parliament, "This isn't the first time our forces have been used for political optics, but it might be the first time the gamble backfired so clearly. The cost of misplaced arrogance has landed at our doorstep."

The ruling party, long reliant on nationalism and militaristic rhetoric, struggled to maintain a coherent position. Attempts to downplay the operation were met with backlash not only from political opponents but also from retired military officers and think tanks who accused the government of politicizing defense without understanding its strategic limits.

Meanwhile, local elections in several states showed a measurable dip in the popularity of the ruling coalition. Public confidence wavered, not only in political leadership but in the ability of state institutions to provide accurate information in moments of crisis.

**Media's Crisis of Credibility**

India's mainstream media, which had long prided itself on patriotic reporting, faced a crisis of credibility. Once the reality of Pakistan's strikes became clear, social media users began compiling and mocking contradictory headlines aired within a span of hours. "From Victory to Silence in 24 Hours" became a trending phrase on Indian Twitter.

A particularly viral clip showed a well-known anchor, previously shouting for "destruction of Pakistan," turning visibly confused as his defense analyst guest admitted on-air that Indian air defenses had failed to detect incoming Pakistani aircraft. This inconsistency wasn't just embarrassing—it was damaging to national morale.

As a result, public trust in traditional media plummeted. Independent journalists and online commentators saw a surge in followership, with audiences now more interested in alternative analyses, satellite verifications, and third-party think tanks than government-aligned news channels.

**The Psychological Toll**

Perhaps the most enduring impact of the operation was psychological. India, accustomed to a posture of escalation and deterrence, was forced into a reactive mode. The myth of invincibility—long cultivated through media, cinema, and political narrative—was challenged by cold, hard facts.

The realization that a coordinated, professional, and restrained operation from Pakistan could expose holes in Indian readiness shook the strategic psyche. Within military circles, analysts began openly discussing the need to reassess assumptions, particularly regarding overreliance on technology and underestimation of adversary capability.

There was also a national identity shock—the emotional dissonance between how India perceived itself and what the operation revealed. For a nation built on the confidence of rising power status, this moment served as a jarring reality check.

**Attempts at Damage Control**

In the weeks following the operation, the Indian government attempted to reassert control over the narrative. It commissioned internal reviews, reshuffled strategic advisers, and launched PR campaigns emphasizing India's broader military capabilities. However, these efforts felt reactive rather than proactive, and failed to fully repair the strategic and psychological damage.

High-level diplomatic outreach began with Western allies, seeking reassurance and support to regain lost standing. Simultaneously, defense deals were hastened in a bid to plug revealed gaps. But the public had already formed its own conclusions—deterrence had failed, and transparency had been lacking.

Operation Bunyan-ul-Marsoos left the Indian media and political establishment grappling with a mirror shattered by unexpected precision and strategic restraint. In this shattered reflection lay the truth: hubris had met its match, not through brute force, but through calculated courage.

The fallout from this operation did not just alter India's external strategy—it sparked a deep and ongoing internal reckoning that may shape its defense and media policies for years to come.

## Global Reassessment of South Asian Dynamics

The execution and outcome of Operation Bunyan-ul-Marsoos marked a defining moment not only for Pakistan and India but also for the broader geopolitical landscape. For decades, the international community viewed South Asia through the lens of a delicate nuclear balance, where tensions often escalated rhetorically but de-escalated diplomatically. However, Pakistan's measured and effective military response—coordinated across conventional, cyber, and information domains—forced global powers to reexamine their assumptions about regional power dynamics, military balance, and diplomatic engagement.

## Challenging the Regional Status Quo

Before this operation, India was largely perceived as the dominant conventional force in South Asia. Backed by significant defense imports, partnerships with the West, and a robust media narrative, India was seen as the regional hegemon in waiting. Pakistan, by contrast, was often viewed through a narrower frame of nuclear deterrence and asymmetric warfare.

Operation Bunyan-ul-Marsoos disrupted that perception. Pakistan displayed not only military precision and multi-branch integration but also a level of strategic maturity that caught many foreign observers off guard. The ability to respond forcefully while maintaining escalation control introduced a new layer of respect for Pakistan's military establishment among global security analysts.

This forced countries like the United States, China, Russia, and key European powers to revisit their South Asia policy frameworks, particularly in areas of arms sales, strategic dialogues, and intelligence cooperation.

## Washington's Calculated Silence

In Washington, the response was notable for its silence during the operation and measured statements afterward. The U.S., traditionally inclined to offer support to India as a counterweight to China, found itself in a difficult position. On one hand, it wanted to avoid escalating tensions between two nuclear states; on the other, it could not ignore the competence and restraint Pakistan demonstrated.

Analysts in the Pentagon and State Department viewed Pakistan's success not just as a military achievement, but as proof that Islamabad could be a rational, responsible actor in a high-stakes conflict. This led to renewed discussions on strategic engagement with Pakistan, particularly in counterterrorism, cyber security, and conflict de-escalation protocols.

## China's Strategic Smile

China, a long-time ally of Pakistan, observed the operation with strategic satisfaction. The demonstration of Pakistan's conventional capabilities against India bolstered China's regional posture without requiring direct involvement. Chinese analysts praised Pakistan's blend of conventional military strength, information warfare, and diplomatic restraint, viewing it as a stabilizing counterweight to India's increasingly assertive foreign policy.

There were also indirect gains for China's Belt and Road Initiative (BRI), as stability in Pakistan reinforced confidence in Chinese investments in the China-Pakistan Economic Corridor (CPEC). Discussions emerged within Chinese think tanks regarding joint air defense systems and military integration, with a particular focus on electronic warfare and surveillance collaboration.

## Russia's Balancing Act

Russia, traditionally seen as a defense partner of India, found itself walking a tightrope. While it could not publicly criticize India, Moscow quietly acknowledged the vulnerabilities exposed in Indian systems—many of which were supplied by Russia itself, including the S-400 air defense systems.

Russian defense experts admitted, albeit cautiously, that doctrinal rigidity and over-reliance on technology had weakened India's tactical response. As a result, Russian diplomats began reaching out more actively to Pakistan, discussing non-lethal defense cooperation, regional security dialogues, and even potential energy collaboration. The operation had thus widened Pakistan's strategic space.

## European and Middle Eastern Engagement

In Europe, the reaction was analytical. NATO-affiliated think tanks published papers detailing the implications of Pakistan's success, particularly its effective use of cyber warfare and information control. The operation became a case study in how modern militaries could leverage precision over volume, and restraint over bravado.

In the Middle East, key partners like Saudi Arabia, UAE, and Turkey publicly supported Pakistan's right to self-defense and privately expressed interest in military cooperation. There was a marked uptick in defense discussions, joint training exercises, and high-level visits between military officials in the months following the operation.

## United Nations and Strategic Neutrality

At the UN, Pakistan's diplomatic performance post-operation was widely praised. The presentation of evidence, clarity of purpose, and calls for de-escalation helped counter India's narrative and positioned Pakistan as the more responsible actor in global forums. This credibility boost led to stronger voices advocating for Pakistan's inclusion in international conflict resolution platforms and non-proliferation dialogues.

The operation also renewed calls among UN observers and peace institutes to reassess South Asia's conflict resolution mechanisms, emphasizing the need for neutral mediation structures to address future flare-ups before they escalate.

## A New Strategic Equation

Operation Bunyan-ul-Marsoos was more than a tactical success—it was a strategic inflection point. It reshaped how the world views military balance in South Asia. Pakistan, long viewed as reactive or dependent on nuclear leverage, emerged as a multi-dimensional power capable of calculated, integrated warfare.

For global powers, the operation signaled the need to engage South Asia with greater nuance and less bias. For Pakistan, it opened new doors in defense diplomacy. And for the region, it introduced a new reality: the era of unchallenged assumptions is over.

# Chapter 12
# Lessons for the Future

As the echoes of Operation Bunyan-ul-Marsoos faded from the skies, what remained was not just a sense of victory but a deeper understanding of how warfare, strategy, and national resolve had evolved. This operation, born in urgency but executed with precision and restraint, offered Pakistan more than a moment of triumph—it provided a blueprint for the future. From military doctrine to public unity, from cyber command to international diplomacy, the mission revealed where the nation was strong—and where it must grow stronger still.

The greatest takeaway from this operation was the power of measured force. Pakistan proved that a disciplined, proportionate response could achieve strategic objectives without triggering uncontrollable escalation. By avoiding emotional overreaction, the nation redefined deterrence—not through brute strength, but through tactical intelligence, moral clarity, and operational excellence.

Equally important were the technological and tactical innovations deployed during the operation. From real-time intelligence sharing and precision-guided strikes to coordinated electronic warfare and cyber disruption, Pakistan displayed a modern and adaptive fighting force. These successes must now be institutionalized, studied, and built upon—not as isolated achievements, but as integrated components of future defense architecture.

Finally, the mission highlighted the urgent need to strengthen national defense policy holistically—including civil defense, strategic communication, and internal unity. Deterrence in the 21st century is not just about weapons; it's about perception, credibility, and resilience. Pakistan must invest in doctrine, training, and the development of next-generation systems—while fostering a society that remains calm and confident in the face of conflict.

This chapter explores these lessons in detail, not just as a retrospective, but as a strategic guidepost for policymakers, military planners, and citizens. Because if Bunyan-ul-Marsoos was the test, then what comes next is the responsibility of preparing wisely for tomorrow.

## The Power of Measured Force

In the annals of modern warfare, victory is not always defined by destruction, but by precision, timing, and discipline. Operation Bunyan-ul-Marsoos offered a striking example of how measured force—deployed thoughtfully and strategically—can produce results far more lasting than sheer aggression. In a region prone to volatile escalations and deeply rooted animosities, Pakistan's choice to respond with calculated restraint reshaped both the tactical battlefield and the psychological space in which deterrence lives.

## Restraint as a Strategic Weapon

Measured force is not weakness; it is a mark of military and moral maturity. In this operation, Pakistan demonstrated a level of composure that surprised both its adversaries and global observers. Instead of launching widespread retaliation or sabre-rattling, Pakistan chose limited, high-value, and time-sensitive targets, each selected for its military significance and symbolic weight. These strikes were coordinated not to humiliate, but to send a clear message: Pakistan has the capacity, the intelligence, and the resolve to defend its sovereignty—without destabilizing the region.

This form of restraint had a dual effect. Internally, it galvanized national pride without inciting fear. Citizens did not see a nation bent on war, but one ready to defend itself with dignity. Externally, it projected Pakistan as a responsible nuclear state—one that understands the weight of escalation and opts for stability without surrender.

## Precision Over Excess

Traditionally, military might has been equated with volume—more firepower, more troops, more destruction. However, the post-9/11 battlefield has evolved. Asymmetric warfare, hybrid conflict, and cyber capabilities have demanded smarter approaches. Operation Bunyan-ul-Marsoos thrived within this paradigm. Rather than aiming for territorial gains or large-scale destruction, Pakistan's forces executed targeted precision strikes, disrupting enemy capabilities while avoiding unnecessary collateral damage.

For example, Pakistani airstrikes deliberately avoided civilian population centers, striking logistics hubs, radar stations, and missile storage sites. This minimized human casualties while maximizing strategic disruption. It also neutralized India's expected propaganda narrative of "Pakistani aggression," as the precision and focus of the strikes made it impossible to frame the operation as reckless or indiscriminate.

### Credibility Without Escalation

Perhaps the greatest achievement of measured force is that it enhances credibility while reducing the risk of uncontrolled conflict. Had Pakistan overreacted, it would have played into India's hands, potentially drawing global condemnation and escalating into a broader war. Instead, the operation was executed with such clarity and calm that even India's international allies were forced to acknowledge Pakistan's self-restraint.

This approach also restored confidence in Pakistan's military doctrine. It showed that the armed forces were not only battle-ready but doctrinally sound—that decisions were being made not in the heat of emotion but from principled, well-calibrated command structures. This reassertion of control and competence sent a lasting message: deterrence works best when backed by intelligence, not impulse.

### Psychological Dominance

Military engagements are not only physical contests; they are also battles for perception. Operation Bunyan-ul-Marsoos succeeded in tilting the psychological playing field. The use of measured force made India appear reactionary and unprepared, while Pakistan's cool-headed operation framed it as the rational actor in an irrational moment.

This had cascading effects. Indian media, accustomed to chest-thumping, found itself embarrassed by conflicting reports and a lack of real-time information. Indian political leadership, which had staked much on its image of regional dominance, now had to grapple with a domestic audience demanding answers. By contrast, Pakistan's narrative was tight, confident, and internationally credible—a rare and powerful shift in psychological dominance.

## Lessons for the Doctrine

The success of measured force must now be internalized into Pakistan's long-term defense doctrine. The operation showed that military effectiveness doesn't always require a show of brute strength. It requires clarity of purpose, operational discipline, real-time intelligence, and controlled execution.

Training programs, simulations, and strategic planning must now revolve around this evolved doctrine. The future of conflict, particularly in South Asia, is unlikely to involve large-scale wars; instead, it will involve brief, high-stakes confrontations where perception, precision, and restraint will determine the victor—not just the number of bombs dropped.

Furthermore, diplomatic arms of the state must learn to leverage measured force in foreign relations. When the military speaks in restraint and precision, diplomats are given stronger cards at negotiation tables. The image of Pakistan as a mature, measured state enhances its position in global forums—from the UN Security Council to regional alliances and beyond.

## A New Gold Standard

In essence, the power of measured force is the power of confidence. Operation Bunyan-ul-Marsoos set a new standard for how a modern state can assert its red lines without igniting a regional inferno. It proved that in today's world, restraint is not the opposite of power—it is a more sophisticated, sustainable, and effective form of it.

By choosing precision over provocation, and clarity over chaos, Pakistan emerged not just stronger, but wiser—a lesson that must now shape the soul of its national defense thinking for decades to come.

## Building on Technological and Tactical Success

Operation Bunyan-ul-Marsoos was not just a demonstration of bravery—it was a masterclass in technological application and tactical execution. It marked a moment when Pakistan's defense establishment fused modern tools with timeless principles of warfare, achieving strategic results with minimal risk. From precision airstrikes and electronic warfare to synchronized operations across multiple defense branches, the operation reflected years of quiet evolution within the armed forces. But success is not an end point—it's a foundation. The true challenge now lies in building on this achievement and shaping it into a permanent institutional advantage.

### The Triumph of Precision Technology

At the core of Bunyan-ul-Marsoos was the effective use of advanced military technology. Precision-guided munitions, real-time satellite imaging, and unmanned aerial vehicles (UAVs) played a critical role. These technologies allowed Pakistan to strike selectively at high-value Indian military assets while avoiding collateral damage—a tactical and moral win.

For instance, drone surveillance enabled Pakistani planners to confirm enemy activity and movement in near real-time. The coordination between ground intelligence and airborne assets shortened the decision-making loop, increasing both speed and accuracy. This intelligence-to-action cycle must now be embedded into everyday military operations.

Moreover, the electronic warfare (EW) teams demonstrated their ability to jam enemy communications and radar systems temporarily, giving Pakistan's Air Force a critical edge. This success proved that non-kinetic capabilities, such as EW and cyber tools, can be just as decisive as firepower in modern conflicts.

**Institutionalizing Tactical Coordination**

Perhaps more impressive than the hardware was the tactical coordination between Pakistan's Army, Air Force, Navy, and Intelligence services. This jointness ensured seamless operation across air, land, and digital domains. Command centers communicated fluidly, intelligence was shared without bureaucratic delays, and decision-making was decentralized enough to be agile.

This type of integration should now be formalized through joint operations doctrine, standardized command protocols, and a national military database that connects every arm of the defense apparatus. War games and simulations must be redesigned to reflect hybrid warfare, where information dominance is just as important as physical force.

Furthermore, the military should establish a permanent cyber command structure, fully resourced and integrated with other arms of the state. The future battlefield will be shaped by data, networks, and digital disruption—this operation was only the beginning.

## Investing in Indigenous Defense Technologies

One of the most important takeaways from the operation is the necessity of self-reliance in defense technology. While foreign procurement will always have its place, long-term strategic advantage lies in building indigenous capabilities. Pakistan's defense sector must now prioritize research and development in key areas such as drone manufacturing, AI-based reconnaissance tools, stealth technology, and cybersecurity infrastructure.

The success of Bunyan-ul-Marsoos highlighted the value of tailored, locally adapted systems that can respond to unique regional challenges. This means encouraging public-private partnerships, funding university-level military innovation, and fostering a culture of inter-agency technological collaboration.

It is time to view Pakistan's defense ecosystem not as a set of isolated silos but as an innovation pipeline—where ideas are tested, technologies are refined, and solutions are scaled quickly.

## Modern Training and Talent Development

Technology alone does not win wars—people do. The operation was a testament to the skill, adaptability, and courage of Pakistani personnel. However, to build on this success, the armed forces must now invest even more in training and leadership development.

Future officers must be trained not just in traditional battlefield tactics, but in cyber warfare, drone strategy, psychological operations, and artificial intelligence. Military academies should revise their curricula to reflect 21st-century threats and tools. Exchange programs with technologically advanced nations can accelerate learning, but local war colleges must become think tanks in their own right.

Additionally, integrating civilian talent—particularly in cyber and tech fields—into defense operations can enhance capabilities. The digital battlefield requires not only soldiers but also software engineers, analysts, linguists, and digital strategists.

**Building Strategic Infrastructure**

A key enabler of Operation Bunyan-ul-Marsoos was access to strategic infrastructure—airfields, radar systems, communication links, and mobile command units. The government must now accelerate the development and protection of these assets. Redundancy must be built into communication systems, alternate command centers must be established, and key military bases must be hardened against both kinetic and cyber threats.

Equally important is data security. The operation highlighted how control over information—both in offensive and defensive terms—can shift the outcome of engagements. Data centers, cloud-based intelligence, and protected satellite communication networks must be scaled up and safeguarded with urgency.

**Turning Success into Strategy**

Operation Bunyan-ul-Marsoos was a proof of concept—that Pakistan's armed forces can engage a superior enemy with intelligence, coordination, and restraint. But the mission's greatest value lies not in the immediate outcome, but in the model it provides for the future.

To maintain this edge, Pakistan must treat its military not just as a defense mechanism, but as a technological institution—one that evolves, adapts, and leads. That means permanent investments, agile reforms, and a unified vision. The future of warfare is already here, and Pakistan must not only keep pace—but set the standard.

# Strengthening National Defense Policy

The success of Operation Bunyan-ul-Marsoos was not an accident. It was the result of preparation, coordination, and strategic clarity. Yet, it also exposed the areas where Pakistan's national defense policy needs urgent refinement. In an increasingly unpredictable world—defined by hybrid warfare, cyber threats, and shifting global alliances—defense is no longer just about battlefield tactics. It is about how a nation structures its institutions, aligns its civilian and military priorities, and prepares for both visible and invisible wars. The operation must now serve as a turning point for strengthening Pakistan's defense policy at the national level.

## From Event-Based Reaction to Strategic Continuity

One of the greatest risks facing developing defense structures is an over-reliance on reactive measures. Historically, Pakistan's defense decisions have often been in response to immediate threats or crises, rather than emerging from a long-term strategic vision. While the country has successfully defended its sovereignty time and again, the cost of short-term thinking is high.

Operation Bunyan-ul-Marsoos must mark a shift from reactive doctrine to proactive policy. That means creating a multi-decade national defense strategy, updated regularly, and supported by parliamentary consensus. Such a strategy should outline the development of conventional forces, nuclear doctrine, cyber capabilities, and internal security frameworks in tandem, not isolation.

Pakistan must move from event-based responses to institutional readiness—where national security is a permanent, evolving priority rather than a fluctuating concern.

## Civil-Military Policy Integration

A modern defense policy cannot be the exclusive domain of the military. Civilian institutions play an essential role in both preparing for and managing conflict. In Operation Bunyan-ul-Marsoos, the effectiveness of media control, diplomatic responses, and public messaging highlighted the importance of civil-military synchronization.

Going forward, there must be a national-level security council that is empowered, resourced, and free from political cycles. This body should consist of defense chiefs, intelligence heads, senior ministers, cyber experts, economists, and public health specialists. Because in today's world, national security is multidimensional—a cyber breach, a media leak, or even a public health failure can compromise a nation's defense posture.

## Defense Budget and Resource Allocation

Strengthening defense policy also means rethinking how and where resources are allocated. Pakistan's defense budget must reflect modern realities. Traditional spending on infantry and heavy equipment must now be balanced with investments in technology, research, and cyber infrastructure. Funds should also be directed toward defense education, satellite systems, secure communications, and cross-border intelligence gathering.

Moreover, every rupee spent must be accountable. Transparent procurement policies, partnerships with local defense manufacturers, and third-party audits can improve efficiency. Defense spending should not be a political taboo—it should be a topic of national importance, debated and understood by all stakeholders.

## Doctrine Development and Public Understanding

Military doctrines shape not just strategies but also public expectations. Pakistan's armed forces must now develop, communicate, and update clear doctrines of engagement—what constitutes a red line, how responses are calibrated, and what forms of aggression will be countered with what type of force.

These doctrines must be designed with clarity and broadcast responsibly so that the public, media, and international observers understand Pakistan's security posture. Ambiguity might benefit nuclear deterrence, but in conventional or hybrid warfare, clarity ensures credibility.

Equally important is public education. National defense policy should not remain in the shadows. Schools, universities, and media outlets should promote civic defense awareness—helping citizens understand the role they play in national resilience, from cyber hygiene to misinformation resistance.

## Strengthening Internal Security and Resilience

External threats are only one part of the equation. A robust defense policy must also address internal cohesion and resilience. During Operation Bunyan-ul-Marsoos, the absence of public panic, the trust in armed forces, and the alignment of civilian behavior with national interest were critical assets. These were not incidental; they reflected years of building public confidence.

To maintain this, internal security forces—such as Rangers, FC, and civilian police—must be trained to respond not only to terrorism but to information warfare, civil unrest, and urban sabotage. National drills, scenario planning, and public response exercises should become routine.

Furthermore, legislation related to national defense, cybersecurity, and counter-intelligence must be reviewed and modernized to address evolving threats. A state's ability to act quickly in a crisis often depends on the legal readiness of its institutions.

**Toward a Whole-of-Nation Approach**

Strengthening Pakistan's national defense policy is not just a military project—it is a whole-of-nation undertaking. It requires the involvement of policymakers, civil society, academia, technology sectors, and the common citizen. Operation Bunyan-ul-Marsoos has shown what is possible when national purpose is unified. Now, that momentum must be institutionalized.

The mission's success must lead to a redefined defense policy— one that sees war not as an anomaly, but as a condition for which the nation is always prepared. One that prioritizes technological superiority, civic unity, doctrinal clarity, and strategic foresight.

Because in the modern era, victory belongs not to those who respond first—but to those who prepare best.

www.ingramcontent.com/pod-product-compliance
Lightning Source LLC
LaVergne TN
LVHW061528070526
838199LV00009B/412